Dimes to Dollars

Collecting Baseball Cards

Donn Pearlman

Bonus Books, Chicago

91   90   89   88   87   5   4   3   2   1

Library of Congress Catalog Card Number: 86-72779

International Standard Book Number: 0-933893-30-2

Bonus Books, Inc.
160 East Illinois Street
Chicago, Illinois 60611

Printed in the United States of America

To my son, Russ, who reintroduced me to the wonderful delights of trading cards (both baseball and "Star Wars") and to my wife, Fran, who lovingly puts up with both of us and our toys.

And to Donn Clendenon, first baseman of the 1969 Miracle Mets, whose parents tossed an extra letter on his first name, too.

Contents

ACKNOWLEDGMENTS

This book would not have been possible without the kind assistance of executives from Donruss, Fleer, and Topps. Ladies and gentlemen, please step from the dugout and wave your hats to the crowd; you keep hitting home runs for the collectors ever year.

In addition to those who are specifically mentioned by name in the book, I give special thanks to Dr. James Beckett and Bob Lemke, two collectors who are just as diligent with their superb quality hobby publications as they are with their superb, personal baseball card collections.

Thanks also to fellow numismatist Paul Green, who shared his vast baseball knowledge and his time. His sense of humor also deserves an extra inning of recognition. Another All-Star performer is a gentleman and rare coin dealer, Jim Simek, who shared his baseball card collecting memories while taking some of the photos in this book.

And, of course, I am grateful to my Publisher and Editor at Bonus Books, Inc., who added my name to the line-up and then allowed a few extra innings of time for me to finish the manuscript.

Donn Pearlman
February, 1987

Introduction

What's more than 100 years old, yet is as new as this year?

You probably guessed the answer, since you are reading this book. It's baseball cards, of course.

Cards with pictures of popular baseball players first appeared more than a century ago. For generation after generation since then, sports fans have been collecting and swapping cards, talking about the players shown on them, and having lots of fun doing it.

But today, baseball cards are not just fun to collect and trade with friends. They can be investments. Cards that cost a few pennies or a dime when they were issued a few years ago can be worth many dollars each today.

A few of them actually are worth much more than their weight in gold!

Many of these colorful pieces of cardboard are almost like diamonds, rare coins or valuable postage stamps. Baseball cards now are something like Wall Street stock certificates—they each have specific values and they are being bought and sold every day.

Yet, unlike many other kinds of investments in which people must spend hundreds or even thousands of dollars to get started, baseball card collecting can begin with pocket change and probably costs less than a candy bar, a comic book, or a bus ride downtown.

It begins with buying a package of baseball cards purchased at the corner store, the supermarket, a baseball card shop, or wherever these items are sold in your neighborhood.

However, it is not a good idea to buy and sell cards *only* with the idea that you will make money from these activities. You should be a *collector,* rather than just an investor.

Many collectors and investors have made big profits from baseball cards, but that does not automatically mean that the market for cards will continue to explode. Just because a card has increased in value every year for a few years does not mean it will continue to go up in price. As you will read in this book, sometimes the values drop sharply.

As you'll read in later chapters, the relatively new baseball card market and the well-established numismatic and philatelic fields are similar in many ways. If the card market follows the usual patterns of demand for rare coins and postage stamps there will be up and down cycles every three to five years or so. Values will increase, decrease, and hold steady as interest in specific areas of the marketplace changes over the years.

Therefore, to get the most satisfaction—fun—from cards, you should enjoy them for their own sake, not just as some scheme to make money. You should collect. Learn about the cards, the players, and the teams. Be a *collector-investor.* It is the best of both worlds.

Prominent rare coin dealer Q. David Bowers of New Hampshire sells items that range in price from a few dollars to a world's record price of $725,000 for a single gold coin his company sold at an auction. But no matter what the cost of the items he offers, Bowers emphasizes to his customers: "Learn something about them."

The solid advice Bowers provides in his successful book *High Profits from Rare Coin Investment* is as true for baseball cards as it is for coins: "Persons who have made the most consistent profits have been those who have known the most."

As card collector and sportswriter Paul Green of Wisconsin points out: "Baseball cards may be a century old, but the hobby is still immature." The formal marketplace where cards are bought and sold is still being formed, still growing quickly. Opportunities abound.

This book will briefly tell you about the fascinating history of baseball cards and it will tell you the insiders' secrets of collecting them with an eye on investment. You'll be able to have fun and perhaps make some money at the same time.

Not bad for a hobby or spare time activity!

The Warm-Up

When you think about baseball cards do you also think about bubble gum? Many people probably think the two automatically go together; after all, when you buy a pack of baseball cards at the corner store, depending on the brand, a thin slab of pink bubble gum is usually inside the wax paper package.

A hundred years ago it was not chewing gum that accompanied the card; it was tobacco. The early baseball cards were included with cigarettes.

The American League was organized in 1901, but the first "tobacco" cards were issued about 20 years before that time. The photographs on the cards were crude by today's standards. The photos were taken in an artist's studio with the action depicted in the photo simulated to make it look as though the picture actually had been taken at a game.

The baseball that the pictured player was supposed to be catching or hitting really was suspended on a string. The player who appeared to be sliding into a base actually was sliding to a base that was on a wooden floor in the studio.

These nostalgic and sometimes valuable cards have survived much longer than the cigarette brands with which they were issued a century ago. But the names of the tobacco companies—such as Turkey Red and Old Judge—live on with collectors. Although these cigarette brands vanished from store shelves decades ago, their names still bring joy to many sophisticated baseball card collectors.

Goodwin & Co., makers of Old Judge cigarettes, started the pattern of regularly issuing cards back in 1886. The company produced several thousand different cards with photographs of baseball players and other sports celebrities. These cards were smaller than today's typical issues, only $1^1/2$ inches by $2^1/2$ inches, but they became very popular.

Soon several other tobacco companies began offering sports cards with their cigarette packages. Sometimes the cards had photos of the players, sometimes they were drawings.

A few companies, looking to beat the competition, made huge cards nearly a half-foot tall. These are called "cabinet cards" or "cabinets," presumably because they are as big as one. "Cabinets" issued by Turkey Red cigarettes are very popular.

As competition grew among the tobacco firms, and other companies such as Cracker Jack began issuing cards, additional changes occurred. Ornate designs were put on some cards, one or two colors were added to the players' pictures or drawings, and information about the players' statistics was printed on the cards. A Cracker Jack card of Ty Cobb—who hit .400 or more during three seasons of his 24-year baseball career—appears on the front cover of this book.

It may be hard to imagine a regular baseball card that is not in full color and does not include stats about the player. What we take for granted with today's cards were novelties when they were first introduced years ago.

Although the cigarette companies were not actually the first to produce baseball cards—there is still some mystery and controversy over who made those first cards back in the mid-1800s—they did establish the trend.

These 19th century cards are still eagerly bought and sold by collectors; however, trying to put together a superb, mint condition set can be impossible or expensive. Or both.

One of the most expensive baseball cards you can buy today was issued during those early days of the cigarette card promotions. In fact, because this particular card was issued by a tobacco company is the reason it is so expensive.

In 1910, Hall of Fame shortstop John Peter Wagner, known as "Honus Wagner, the flying Dutchman," demanded that his baseball card be withdrawn by the tobacco company issuing it because he did not endorse the use of tobacco. He did not smoke and he did not want anyone influenced to smoke just because his picture in a Pittsburgh uniform appeared on a card issued by a cigarette company.

A few of these baseball cards did reach the public. Even though these are certainly not the rarest cards—several dozen are known to exist—the Honus Wagner cards certainly are the most expensive. In top condition they have sold for as much as $25,000 each and rate the unofficial title, "King of Cards."

Why? Perhaps because of the colorful story about Wagner's anti-smoking efforts. Perhaps because of the early publicity about the cards being withdrawn. But the basic reason for the high cost of the Wagner card, and the value of *any* baseball card, is that someone is willing to pay a certain price for it.

If a card is offered for $100 and no one wants to buy it, after a while the price usually will start to drop, down to $90 or $85, until someone buys it. On the other hand, if there is a sudden, big demand for those cards at $100 each, then the sellers quickly will raise their prices, up to $110 or $125.

Not all turn-of-the-century cards are expensive. Some of the more common cigarette cards, in worn condition, are available for just a few dollars each.

In addition to the Cracker Jack Company (the same Cracker Jack you enjoy now), other candy makers began producing sports cards. Many companies started issuing them in the 1920s.

Today many different food companies provide customers with various kinds of baseball cards. A few of them that have printed cards recently: Wheaties, Kellogg's, Pepsi, Squirt, Hostess, Drake's Bakery, Mother's Cookies, Jay's Potato Chips, Ralston Purina, and Burger King. Individual stores or store chains may also issue baseball cards. Recent examples include True Value, Walgreen's, Woolworth's, K-Mart and Kay-Bee Toys.

"King of Cards"—the famous Honus Wagner tobacco card (T-206); not the rarest, but certainly the most expensive baseball card.
(Krause Publications Photo)

Sometimes these cards are issued nationwide. Sometimes they are only available at the time of issue in one part of the country. When the cards are not issued nationwide they are called "regionals."

A nationwide company may produce different sets of cards to be issued in different parts of the country. Padres cards would be distributed regionally in the San Diego area, while the company's Twins cards would be made available around Minneapolis-St. Paul.

The term "regional" is a little deceptive. Because of the huge dealer and collector network that has been established, most regionally-issued items are easily available everywhere, either at local card shops and weekend card shows or through mail-order dealers.

Back in the 1920s a Chicago company started a new trend by selling baseball cards through vending machines. For one cent you could purchase a postcard-sized baseball card from one of the amusement arcade devices made by the Exhibit Supply Co.

The modern era of baseball cards began during the Great Depression. The Goudey Gum Co. of Boston produced a series of

239 colorful baseball cards in 1933. Each card portrayed a full-color line drawing of a player.

The cards quickly became popular, and why not? In that 1933 set you'll find more than three dozen Hall of Fame players. There are even four different cards that year depicting the great Babe Ruth.

Other chewing gum companies quickly entered the market with their own cards. One of them, Gum Products, Inc., issued several popular series of cards that were produced in black and white.

Other baseball card makers during the 1930s included the National Chicle Co. and the DeLong Gum Co. The names of their baseball card sets often were as colorful as the cards themselves: "Diamond Stars," "Double Play," and "Batter Up" are some of the names given to card sets produced during those years.

When the United States entered World War II late in 1941 citizens were urged to conserve such items as meat, rubber, and paper. These were goods needed for the country's war effort. Because of the paper shortage the gum companies halted production of baseball cards.

The war ended in 1945, but baseball card production did not resume until 1948. Gum Products, Inc. became Bowman Gum, Inc., and the company began selling packs containing one black and white baseball card accompanied by a piece of bubble gum for one cent. Forty-eight different cards were produced for the 1948 set.

The Stan Musial card (#36) that originally was available for a penny now sells for about $100 in mint condition.

In 1949 Bowman expanded its efforts and produced 240 different cards—and in color. The addition of color tinting may have been due to increasing competition. The Leaf Company issued nearly 100 color cards in 1948 and 1949.

Bowman continued making cards through the 1955 baseball season. The largest Bowman set during those years is the 1951 series of 324 cards. Among the rookies making their first major league appearances that year were Willie Mays (#305) and Mickey Mantle (#253).

An interesting aspect of the 1955 Bowman set is that it contains more than 30 cards honoring umpires. Five players' cards

*Jim Honochick, one
of the 31 baseball
umpire cards (#267)
issued as part of the
1955 Bowman "tv set."*
(Krause Publications Photo)

also contained major errors—either the wrong player's photo was shown or the name of the player was misspelled.

The error cards are interesting, but not very valuable. In fact, the cards issued later with the correct spellings or photos are worth a few dollars more than the cards containing the mistakes.

Many of these cards from the 1955 Bowman set are available for a dollar or less in mint condition. However, the mint Mickey Mantle (#202) and Ernie Banks (#242) cards usually sell for $50 to $75 each.

The growing influence of television was easily seen in the last set of Bowman baseball cards. The border around each player's photograph made it look as though he was on television. Collectors often refer to this particular series of 320 cards as the "tv set."

The same year that Bowman issued its largest set, 1951, a new competitor entered the marketplace. Topps Chewing Gum Inc. of Brooklyn, New York, produced a set of 52 somewhat plain-looking cards. Actually there were two series of 52 cards, one series with a red back, the other with blue.

But the next year Topps issued a 407 card set that has become a collectors' classic. The 1952 Topps set established a new standard for attractiveness and a slightly larger size card than the ones issued by Bowman. Even a very worn '52 Topps set commands more than $1,000, yet collectors can purchase mint condition examples of the common cards from this set for less than $10 each.

These sets are so popular that "reprints" of the cards have been produced and sell for $35 to $45 per set. There are also reproductions of the 1911 Turkey Red, 1915 Cracker Jack, 1934 Goudy, 1940s Play Ball series, and 1953 Bowman sets. Other sets and even individual cards, for example the Pete Rose 1963 Topps rookie card, have been issued in recent years. Some of them are authorized reprints and clearly marked "copy," others have been produced illegally and must be considered counterfeits.

Topps Chewing Gum Inc. has regularly issued cards every year since 1951. Topps purchased Bowman Gum Co. in early 1956, and the Topps card set that year is the first to contain a checklist of available players' cards in that year's set.

Other Topps' innovations since then include the first cards featuring All-Star selections, rookie All-Stars, "game action" photos, and additional player statistics such as stolen bases and pitching shutouts. To meet the growing demand for baseball cards, Topps began making the entire series of the year's cards available from the beginning of the baseball season in 1974. Topps first produced "traded" sets in 1974 and 1976, then began regularly issuing them in 1981.

Now, several of the major card companies introduce their latest cards during the Winter, months before Spring training camps are even open.

Traditionally, the photos of players that appeared on cards of the past few decades were taken during Spring training. More and more photos now are taken during the regular baseball season at the major league stadiums.

"Several different types of photos are taken of each ballplayer. Action pictures are taken, as well as posed portraits. The pictures are taken from different angles with players wearing their caps and without them," explains Topps' spokesman Norman J. Liss.

"The players' statistics listed on the back of each of our cards are compiled by the staff of the Topps sports department from the official league records."

The Fleer Corp. of Philadelphia entered the baseball card

Hall of Famer and sports broadcaster Lou Boudreau was among those depicted (#16) in the 1960 Fleer "Baseball Greats" series.
(James A. Simek Photo)

market in 1959 with an 80 card set commemorating the accomplishments of superhero Ted Williams. In 1960 Fleer sold a 79 card series depicting other baseball greats. Each photo was slightly tinted to make it resemble the cards issued in the 1930s and earlier.

The "Baseball Greats" format continued in 1961, but then Fleer did not issue any cards the next year.

In 1963 Fleer produced a small set of 66 cards featuring current players. Interestingly, the most valuable card of the set is not that of a player, and it isn't even numbered. Apparently, on the final run of the presses, the Joe Adcock card, then Cleveland first baseman (#46), was replaced with a checklist card. The result: fewer Joe Adcock cards are available than the other 65 players in that year's set, and even fewer unnumbered checklist cards are available.

Although some card quantities were limited, there was no shortage of lawsuits being filed in those days over what company had the rights to produce baseball cards and issue them in packages containing bubble gum. Because of the legal claims and counter-claims those 1963 Fleer cards were sold in packs without any gum. They did contain a cherry-flavored cookie.

One of the scarce cards of the 1963 Fleer set, Cleveland player Joe Adcock (#46).
(Krause Publications Photo)

That was the last set Fleer produced until 1981 when the company reentered the market with 660 new cards. Every year since then Fleer has started the season by issuing 660 cards.

There was no cherry-flavored cookie when Fleer resumed production of baseball cards for the 1981 season, but the company did present collectors with a new way of grouping the cards in the set. Instead of assigning card numbers almost at random Fleer began grouping members of the same team together with consecutive card numbers. The system continues today.

"There was nothing really mysterious about it," admits Donald Peck, president of Fleer Corp. "It simplified things for collectors and gave us an edge over competitors who hadn't thought of it, or for their own reasons didn't want to do it."

In 1982 Fleer introduced another new concept: multiple checklist cards—one for each major league team and special checklists for special cards in the year's set.

"We've done as much as we can to make ourselves distinctive and to be innovative without departing from where the collectors want to be in the hobby. What competition has done is to make the cards considerably better than they were when only one manufacturer was doing them. That's what happens in the real world with competition," Donald Peck points out.

Since the end of the 1984 baseball season, the company annually has produced a set of updated cards to indicate players who've been traded during the regular season and to include rookies not included in the year's regular set.

When the updated sets arrive each Fall they are quickly purchased by collectors through hobby channels, mail-order purchases, or directly from card shops.

"The hobby channels have become a very, very important part of the total market and we pay attention to them. They're a real eye-opener," says Peck.

The Donruss Co., a division of Leaf, Inc. of Bannockburn, Illinois, entered the card game in 1981. Donruss has been producing large sets of "regular size" cards every year since then and also makes specialty items such as pop-up cards and puzzles. (Other specialty items, such as the Topps 3-D "Baseball Stars" photo cards, have been introduced to the market.)

The Donruss Company entered the baseball card marketplace in a big way in 1981 with 605 players and checklist cards. It was the direct result of the Fleer Corp. winning a federal lawsuit against Topps over the rights to produce and market cards. The ruling, in the Federal District Court in Philadelphia, broke Topps' monopoly.

When the case was appealed by Topps, the federal appellate court dampened the Fleer victory by ruling that only Topps had the right to market baseball cards with a confectionary product (traditionally bubble gum) or market the cards alone without anything else in the package.

If other manufacturers obtain permission to produce baseball cards from Major League Baseball (to use team names, logos and colors) and permission from the Players' Association (to use the players' names and likenesses) the cards must be accompanied by something inside the package—an "inpack"—and that something must not be a confectionary product.

That's why Donruss card packs include Hall of Fame jigsaw puzzle pieces, and why Fleer has logo stickers. The Donruss Co. has an exclusive agreement with The National Baseball Hall of Fame that permits the company to use the Hall of Fame logo. Also,

This 1983 card (#3)
of "Mr. October,"
Reggie Jackson, is an
example of the pop-
ular Donruss "Di-
amond Kings" cards
drawn by sports
illustrator Dick Perez.
(James A. Simek Photo)

Donruss has an agreement to depict the names and likenesses of specific Hall of Fame members.

The "Diamond Kings" series of 26 annual cards that Donruss began issuing in 1982 has become very popular among collectors, and it has developed a "cult" following among determined autograph collectors. Each card is a reproduction of original artwork by well-known sports illustrator, artist and designer Dick Perez depicting current kings of the baseball diamond. Perez is the official artist for The Donruss Co. and the National Baseball Hall of Fame.

"The reason we created that idea for Donruss is because we are collectors at heart," explains Frank Steele, a consultant to Donruss and a partner in Perez-Steele Galleries of Fort Washington, PA. "We wake up in the morning as collectors; later in the day we become business people involved with cards. But we are collectors at heart and everything we do springs from the soil of our collecting appetites.

"We felt there was a vacuum in baseball cards and we wanted to bring back to today's cards the idea of artwork. We thought the best and fairest way to do it was to have one Diamond King from each of the 26 major league teams. Initially there was some puzzlement over that when a few Eastern-based collectors wondered why we didn't include more members of the Yankees, Mets and Phillies. It was a time when, for example, the Phillies were riding high with Pete Rose, Mike Schmidt, and Steve Carlton. But since Donruss is an international company, marketing all over the United States and Canada, we have to be responsible to the needs of the collectors in Seattle and Texas and Canada. When I was growing up in Pittsburgh, even though some of those Pirates teams were terrible, they were still my heroes.

"So, we select one dominant player each year from each of the 26 teams. Donruss became enamored of the idea and they decided to showcase the cards. Therefore, since 1982, the Diamond Kings are always the first 26 numbered cards issued in each set."

Perez-Steele Galleries has also been producing a limited-edition series of postcard-sized illustrations of Hall of Fame inductees. Selected original watercolors are on display at the National Baseball Hall of Fame and Museum in Cooperstown, New York. Other watercolors are shown at Perez-Steele Galleries, or they can be found in private and corporate collections across the country and abroad.

Other innovations from Perez-Steele and Donruss include "Living Legends" (bonus cards issued in 1984), "Rated Rookies," "Highlights" (end-of-the-season cards first issued in 1985), and "The Rookies" (debuted in 1986).

Steele recalls the origin of the "Highlights" cards: "I thought, 'How can we give people a feel of the just-ended baseball season, a pictorial review of the highlights of the season?' So we did 55 different cards and a checklist card and issued them in a flip-top box. A deluxe set with quality, high-gloss printing, gold foil and cellophane wrapped like a deck of playing cards.

"We take the season from opening day to the last day of the regular season. That's the cut-off. We don't extend the set into the playoffs and World Series, otherwise we'd never get the cards out. We track the season and as events occur that we think are significant we log them. We had a complete set of 55 cards by the second week of August. But then, as the season continued, we would replace a previously logged item with the later, more significant event such as someone pitching a perfect no-hitter.

"In 1985, on the last day of the regular season, Phil Niekro hurled his 300th victory, a shutout. That was a monumental feat, so obviously he had to be in the Highlights set and that bumped someone else from the set.

"The criteria we use for selecting players and events for the Highlights set are both objective and subjective judgments. We take the Player of the Month and the Pitcher of the Month from each of the two leagues. We are satisfied that the American and National Leagues have a good overview of who the dominant players are each month. So those automatically are included as four highlights each month. We also take the Most Valuable Player of the All-Star game and recognize him. That's an objective determination, too, because we just use the player voted MVP of the game.

"And starting with the 1986 season we have included the three inductees of that year into the Baseball Hall of Fame as part of the season's highlights," Steele added.

In addition to Topps, Fleer, and Donruss many other firms are making or distributing cards these days. Two of the biggest are The Star Co. of Cherry Hill, New Jersey, and Sportflics of Grand Prairie, Texas. In Canada collectors put together sets produced by O-Pee-Chee Co., Ltd. of London, Ontario, and Donruss-Leaf issues cards in Canada, too. Baseball fans in Japan eagerly buy and sell cards showing their country's top players, and sets have been issued for teams in Venezuela and other countries.

Some manufacturers in the United States have successfully experimented with different forms of cards. Kellogg's used "3-D" special effects starting in 1970, and Topps recently issued large-sized "3-D" cards with the player's face and body raised up above the flat surface of the photo's background. The result looks like a relief map.

Sportflics produces very clever "Magic Motion" cards that change appearance when they are tilted slightly back and forth. Each card is actually three photos in one.

For example, the 1986 card number 97 shows a close-up portrait of New York Mets star Darryl Strawberry. Move the card just a bit and suddenly you see Strawberry at the plate ready to swing the bat. Another tiny flick of the wrist and the Sportflics card shows he has followed through with his powerhouse swing.

Because of the tremendous popularity of baseball cards many

*New York Mets star
Darryl Strawberry in
action on the 1986
Sportflics "Magic
Motion" card (#97).*
(James A. Simek Photos)

companies have printed their own versions and either given them away free or included them as premiums when customers buy their products, such as Kellogg's cereals or Hostess snacks.

Here are a few examples from 1986:

—True Value (hardware store) dealers offered a set of 30 cards.

—Lite Beer sponsored a 22 card set commemorating the 25th anniversary of the Houston Astros that was given away to fans at the Astrodome.

—Spectators attending one of the games of the California Angels at Anaheim Stadium were given sets of 24 "Wildfire Prevention" baseball cards that depicted Smokey the Bear along with favorite players. The sets were sponsored by the California Department of Forestry, the U.S. Forest Service, and the U.S. Department of the Interior. The Angels were "hot" in '86, but they did want to help prevent forest fires.

—Fire prevention was also the theme of a 36 card set issued to commemorate the 10th anniversary of the Toronto Blue Jays. In addition to the usual statistics found on the back of each card there were also fire prevention safety tips.

—Cheerios breakfast cereal offered Canadian customers free baseball cards with the printed information in English and French.

And then, aside from the annual sets of "regular" cards being issued by Topps, Donruss, and Fleer, the companies are making special items: mini-sized and jumbo-sized cards for super star players, puzzle cards, pop-up cards, discs with photos, and others.

Sportflics offered a 50 card set of rookies that included 35 of the 1986 season's top youngsters—such as Jose Canseco and Wally Joyner—and 15 previous Rookie of the Year winners like Fred Lynn, Pete Rose, and Tom Seaver.

Star Company also produced a variety of sets. One of them was a set of 24 cards all featuring Wade Boggs of the Boston Red Sox.

The public's demand for baseball cards keeps the printing presses busy. "Topps sells more than 500-million baseball cards every year," proudly states company spokesman Norman J. Liss.

Topps printed 792 different baseball cards in the regular 1986 season series, then issued a 132 card extended (updated) set. The 1987 regular set again consisted of 792 cards with 694 of them showing different, individual players—the largest number ever in any Topps set. And that is just one company. If you add up all the cards produced by the major companies and all the regional issues from across the country you have literally thousands of different items to collect just to have "one of everything" for that year.

"You could probably go broke just collecting the current year's sets. It would probably cost between two and three thousand dollars to buy one of everything that was produced across the country in 1986," estimates card collector and dealer Steve Gold of AU Sports Memorabilia in Skokie, Illinois. "And even then you probably won't get everything," he added. "Every team puts out their own sets. There are so many regional issues, the special sets, the traded and updated sets—and this is just for the major league teams."

Noted baseball card expert Dr. James Beckett of Dallas believes the huge number of cards issued "has caused people to stop and reflect, and realize they not only cannot get every card that has ever been produced, they may not even be able to obtain one of every card produced this year."

If the strong demand by collectors for even more baseball cards continues, it's likely even more kinds will be produced by these and other businesses.

It is not just the major league teams' and players' sets that attract attention. Many people enjoy assembling complete sets of minor league teams. Some collectors proudly point to these as the very first cards to picture such famous, future Hall of Fame players as Dwight Gooden.

Americans love baseball so much that they cannot live by cards alone. Collectors quickly grab up anything that honors the Great American Pastime. Tokens, medals, coffee mugs, posters—anything with a team emblem or a player's likeness on it is sure to find an eager buyer. Even ceramic cards have been made for collectors. These somewhat fragile collectibles sell for about $10 each and are not the kinds of cards you want to use to toss in rubberband-bound packets on the sidewalk.

Some collectors will pay hundreds of dollars to own the cracked bat of a heavy hitter or a sweat-stained jersey previously worn by some major leaguer. (Late in the 1986 season, Boston outfielder Jim Rice jumped into the third base side lower box seats at Yankee Stadium when a brash fan scooped up Rice's grounded cap. The fan gave back the hat after being chased a few rows by the irate Red Sox star as the box seats area quickly became filled with stadium security guards and a dozen other Boston players.)

Football, hockey, wrestling, golf, soccer, basketball, and Olympic games athletes have been the subjects of sports cards. Over the years quite a few non-sports cards have been issued. The most popular recent issue is "The Garbage Pail Kids." Before that the *Star Wars* movie scenes cards sold millions. "The Bionic Woman," "Magnum, P.I.," "Knight Rider" and "Masters of the Uni-

verse" are some of the hit television shows that have been the subject of cards.

Other non-sports cards have been devoted to the presidents
of the United States.

And if those aren't enough for you, some companies will print
special cards with your own picture on them! You can take your
place in card history along with "Jaws," "Gomer Pyle," and Millard
Fillmore.

This book, however, is devoted to the topic of collecting modern "regular issue" baseball cards—the kind that are packaged in
wax paper or plastic (cellophane) or are available as an entire year
set that comes packed in a long cardboard box.

That narrows the topic somewhat. Yet many different cards
still fit into that category.

The big question you now face is: "What should I collect?"

Getting to First Base

It takes "extra innings" just to list the variety of baseball cards available. Deciding what to collect really isn't that hard, and actually starting a collection is even easier.

"Someone can become a baseball card collector for 35 cents," states Donruss consultant Frank Steele of Perez-Steele Galleries. "You go to a candy store and buy a wax pack and you've got 15 cards. You're not an advanced or major collector, but that's OK because most of us started with just one or two cards. Very few are born with entire collections, and if you are, it probably isn't much fun. The fun is to assemble the collection. That's the fun, the treasure hunt.

"Unlike most other hobbies, there is a marvelous ease-of-entry with baseball cards. If you decided you wanted to collect antique toys, you better have some money, surely more than 35 cents. With baseball cards, whether you are 12 years old by birth or 12 years old by attitude, you can collect today's heroes and today's stars. It keeps you young-at-heart," explains Steele.

Generally, there are two ways to go: Ei-

FIRST ROW: Freese, Face, Swanson, Batboy Vantosky, Thomas, Clemente, Pendleton. SECOND ROW: Smith, Arroyo, Coach Narron, Ass't. Mgr. Sisler, Mgr. Murtaugh, Coach Sukeforth, Coach Levy, O'Brien, Fondy. THIRD ROW: Baker, Pritchard, Mazeroski, Friend, Law, King, Skinner, Douglas, Peterson, Tr. Jorgensen. FOURTH ROW: Trav. Sec'y. Rice, Purkey, Kline, Rand, Foiles, Groat, Smith, Virdon.

PITTSBURGH PIRATES

A quick way to collect "by team"—get all the players on one card such as this 1958 Topps team card (#341) of the Pittsburgh Pirates with a series checklist on the back.

(James A. Simek Photo. Copyright Topps Chewing Gum, Inc.)

ther establish a specific collecting objective, such as all the rookies or all the players on specific teams, and then concentrate your efforts and finances on purchasing those cards—or simply buy a pack of cards and take your chances.

What you collect should be your own decision. Whether you're just in the mood for some hobby fun or you have definite investment goals, you should buy items that are of interest to you. Do certain teams, players or field positions attract your attention? Do you like current rookies or old-time Hall of Famers? Are you a baseball trivia nut? Whatever area appeals to you, go with it. You'll be much happier as a collector than a calculating investor.

The collector spirit should always preside over your activities.

You should feel the pride of ownership, not merely scan the latest price guides to determine if those pieces of cardboard stashed away have gone up in value. Unfortunately, too many card buyers have no idea what's in their hands except that they bought a card for "X" number of dollars yesterday and today they want to sell it for "X plus Y" number of dollars.

Most of the collectors and dealers interviewed for this book recommend that beginning collectors interested in newly-issued cards purchase entire sets at a time. Usually the first shipments of the new cards are made each January, months before the first pitch of Spring training. Sure, buying a full set all at once does eliminate the surprise of opening a fresh, individual pack and discovering what cards you've just acquired. There are, however, advantages to spending $17 to $40 at a time to buy one of everything from a specific card company.

Retail prices for current, complete sets will vary greatly depending on the manufacturer, the demand for their cards, and the time of year the cards are sold. Some sets may increase and others may decrease in value as the baseball season ends depending on the rookie players who have or have not been included in the sets first issued during the year.

For example, the 1986 Donruss sets of 660 cards were offered for only about $18 each at the beginning of the '86 season, but by World Series time they were selling for about $28 per set. One of the main reasons was that the Donruss sets contained a card of red hot rookie Jose Canseco (#39) who was not included by Fleer or Topps until their updated sets were issued late in the season.

Sometimes knowing if a potential rookie is even available for inclusion in a regular set is impossible. For example, the "rookie" card for Kansas City Royals player—and former college football star—Bo Jackson was issued in the 1986 Topps "traded" set.

The updated, extended or traded sets produced by Topps and Fleer for that year each contained 132 cards, and retail prices for them generally were listed by dealers at about $12 when the sets were first released in the Fall. Many dealers who have purchased cases of these sets will divide them and sell individual cards at prices ranging from a few cents to a few dollars, depending on the market for the items.

"My feeling is that young collectors should go for the whole set," says Steve Goldberg of Dalton Stamp & Coin in Dalton, Georgia. In addition to the "Big Three" of Topps, Fleer and Donruss, Goldberg sells many regional baseball card issues such as Drake's Bakeries and products from The Star Company.

"It's one thing if they get the set either as a present or with their own money. It's a good project for the kids to put the sets together themselves. There's too much emphasis when kids want to buy a card on the question of: 'What's it worth?'

"It's important to know what something's worth, but I don't think they should buy only because it's worth 'X' number of dollars, or a card they might like to have that's valued at 25 cents and when they later find out that's all it's worth they don't want it anymore.

"I think they should stick with the major companies. When you start looking at the early Topps cards, well, the kids can't afford those.

"I think that the kids should collect what they want to collect rather than get something because it is what everybody else wants today," Goldberg believes.

"I suggest staying with complete sets, the current sets," recommends dealer Bryan Durta of Munster, Indiana, who specializes in selling cards by complete-set boxes and also deals in wax, cellophane and so-called "rack" packs. He handles the Sportflics and Kellogg's 3-D cards, baseball stickers, and the Canadian O-Pee-Chee cards.

His advice to young collectors about purchasing entire sets at a time also makes good financial sense for adult buyers.

"If you buy a set when it first comes out you're greatly reducing the amount of [financial] risk you're taking. Your best value is in the complete sets. If you buy quantities of a single player's card you're taking a big risk. What if he loses an arm or something?

"If you buy a whole set, and one of the hot players doesn't last too long in the major leagues, you've still got the rest of the players to hold up the value of the set."

What about that most basic question: What to collect?

"It's basically the preference of the collector," explains Durta. "I think there's a lot less risk if they stick with current cards when they first come out. There's a smaller mark-up [retail cost] compared to buying older cards from even a few years earlier, where you're taking a larger risk by paying an already inflated price.

"I don't see as much investment potential in such things as Sportflics or small regional sets, but if they are players or teams that you collect, then that's what you should buy. Most of the items that will go up in value probably will be in the cards from the major sets that come out every year."

Another advocate of purchasing complete sets is dealer Kit Young of Vancouver, Washington, a major, active buyer of modern era baseball cards.

"I'm more conservative. I'm more inclined to go for the Blue Chip stuff, the straight sets. But the main thing is: Collect what you enjoy.

"I think there's too much emphasis on investment. It's kind of fun to watch the prices go up, but the first thing I tell new collectors is, 'Go for something you get a kick out of, something that's a lot of fun.'

"It's supposed to be fun. That's what the hobby is all about. It's not meant to be an investment portfolio like a lot of kids and adults like to view it.

"I personally lean toward the older stuff. I think what kids and many adults don't quite understand is that there is a great quantity of cards being produced today. There are hundreds of thousands of each card of Darryl Strawberry and Don Mattingly. The values on those is getting way out of whack compared to their actual scarcity, or lack of scarcity.

"The stuff that is relatively under-valued is the older stuff from the 1950s and 1960s. You can buy a nice card of Frank Robinson or Al Kaline for $5 or $10 that is a much tougher card to get than a 1984 Darryl Strawberry. A 1962 Kaline goes for less than a 1984 Strawberry. That doesn't make an awful lot of sense.

"The older stuff is a relative bargain compared to the new stuff."

Another fan of "older stuff" is sportswriter Paul Green of Ridgeway, Wisconsin. Although he says it is not "a full-time addiction," Green does enjoy collecting baseball cards and writing professionally about them and about the players whose pictures appear on them. Green's byline appears regularly in such publications as *Sports Collectors Digest*, *Baseball Card News* and *Baseball Cards* magazine. He also is the author of two books about baseball players, *Forgotten Fields* (Parker Publications) and *The Battles of Bunker Hill* (Krause Publications).

"Most people tend to start collecting with the modern issues, and that's fine. I would encourage people to really collect the cards they like and be less concerned about where its value is going to be at a given point down the road," suggests Green.

"Young people today tend to collect the players of this era. Some of my friends, however, would much prefer to go back and put together sets from the 1950s—the kinds of cards we remember that we used to have when we were young, but then our mothers threw out.

"That's the common refrain I hear from friends. To be honest, I've tried to track down my old cards, but there's no trace. I can't say for sure what happened to them. There's a very strong suspicion that when Paul went away to college the cards went away someplace else," laughed Green.

"By and large, those 1950s sets are readily available at reasonably inexpensive prices. If you're going to be budget conscious, I wouldn't be concerned about putting together a set from a specific year, but rather put together sets of your favorite team or teams.

"Among the things you need to know about cards is current prices. I recommend comparing dealers' prices in the major magazines so you have a rough idea of what you should be paying. Fortunately, the financial stakes usually are not high unless you are dealing with rookie cards of some of the major players. I suggest people should not go out and buy $250 baseball cards until they've had some experience in the hobby.

"Just because a baseball card is rare does not make it particularly valuable. You can go back to the cards from the 1930s and early 1940s and the quantity of cards produced is nothing compared to what is being produced these days. But if it is not a big name player from that era then they're not in very much demand and consequently will not bring a higher price than, say, today's hottest rookie card. It is supply and demand. There is a bigger supply of cards today, but the demand is greater," Green points out.

He warns of what he calls "The Franklin Mint Syndrome." During the late 1960s and 1970s, the Franklin Mint of Pennsylvania produced a large quantity of beautifully designed and perfectly struck silver tokens and other silver objects. Even though these were nice collectibles, there eventually was more material available than the market could absorb and the investment value of Franklin Mint products in the secondary (resale) market fell sharply.

Unlike most collectors, Jeff Fritsch of Stevens Point, Wisconsin, didn't have to decide whether or not he would begin collecting. In his family, cards are a way of life.

Jeff's father, Larry Fritsch, has been buying, trading and selling baseball cards since 1948. He began dealing full-time in 1970. His company boasts of having an inventory of more than 32 million cards in stock.

Jeff was born in 1959 and explains with a laugh: "Card collecting is in my blood. As long as I can remember there were cards around. I guess I didn't have any choice unless I wanted to move out of the house at age three."

With all that baseball card experience, does he believe beginners should purchase a whole set quickly, concentrate on the rookies, go for the super stars, or what?

"Our opinion is very strong on that question. We feel they should be [whole] sets. Either buy a complete set from a dealer or go out and put it together from the packs.

"That's what we definitely recommend, but I'm beginning to feel that we're becoming a minority in the hobby. But that's still our opinion on it.

"[Until recently] most of the people buying cards were true collectors. A collector usually is more interested in obtaining as many different possible items instead of trying to get quantities of one certain card.

"If I needed a 1986 'Joe Blow,' I'd much rather have that card than a second Dwight Gooden, although the hobby now is going the other way. Everybody is concerned about buying a card today for a penny then selling it for a buck down the road. But if I, as a collector, buy something for my collection then the last thing on my mind is what the card is going to be worth five years from now, because I don't know if I would ever sell it from my collection anyway," Fritsch admits.

If collectors are going to assemble sets, should they stick with classics or go into regional or more modern cards?

"It comes down to dollars. If you can afford to go out and get every set that's been issued, that's excellent. My opinion, though, is that to start, perhaps you should buy a Topps set first, then if you want to expand a little bit you can buy a Fleer, Donruss or Sportflics set. And then, if you want to expand a little more, you can go into some of the odd sets, such as the Super Stars, the 3-D sets, a regional issue, or dabble in the Star Company.

"That can be decided by the individual collector. Maybe someone living in Wisconsin, for example, may want to specialize in buying Brewers material. Collect everything from the three major sets (Topps, Fleer, and Donruss) and then the collector could buy anything else related to the Brewers and their players.

"I myself would not attempt to go out and get every set that is being issued these years. There are so many local and regional sets being produced now, you might not even be aware of half of them being available," Fritsch says.

Some baseball card dealers offer "starter sets," assortments of cards that, priced as a group, are usually cheaper than purchasing each card separately. These sets or lots often are grouped by card manufacturer and by dates. For example, a dealer may offer 200 different 1968 Topps cards in excellent to mint condition for $25, or 100 different 1954 Bowman cards in very good or better condition for $85. There also are dealer advertisements for complete sets of different manufacturers and different years. These are offered with cards ranging from very good to excellent or even very good-mint condition.

These assortments and sets are an easy way for new collectors to get acquainted with specific card series or to dive into a specific collecting area. It is like stepping up to a buffet table; you can quickly sample many different delights.

There are disadvantages. First, the buyer has only limited control over what cards will be received—the dealer chooses the specific cards. You can't request 200 different 1968 Topps for $25 that include Pete Rose (#230) and Steve Carlton (#408). You also could not specifically request Mickey Mantle (#280). And when purchasing many of those assorted card lots you have to decide if you are collecting or just hoarding baseball cards. Are you assembling a set or merely accumulating?

Second, and very important, the assortment you purchase can include a wide range of card conditions. The dealer can advertise "100 different cards VG-Mint," and when the package arrives you receive only two mint condition cards and 98 others (including any "key" or popular players' cards) with more creases than a Marine's uniform.

When an advertisement indicates the merchandise will be "VG or better," the odds are VG that only a few of the better cards will be better than very good condition.

Purchasing assorted lots of cards can be fun: Anticipating what will arrive and discovering what you own is exciting. But serious collectors who have definite collecting goals usually find that choosing cards one-at-a-time is much more rewarding. And anyone who is more interested in baseball cards as investments rather than as pleasurable collectibles probably should look the other way when offered "investor-quality lots" of hundreds or thousands of assorted cards. Only a handful of major dealers who have the financial resources and the hobby connections to assemble true "investment quality" packages can put together these kinds of portfolios—but you've got to know your dealer. More about that in another chapter.

If you are still undecided about what to collect, do some "window shopping." Browse through the hobby newspapers, magazines and price guides (see the last chapter). Casually talk with a local card dealer about what is available and, if one is nearby, attend a weekend card show and scan the merchandise. Surely you'll hit on something that strikes your fancy, rather than striking out.

A Heavy Hitter

An interview

with

Dr. James

Beckett

J ames Beckett of Dallas, Texas, has an academic background in mathematics and statistics. He has successfully combined his training as a statistician with his long-time love of baseball and baseball cards to produce some of the hobby's most important publications, including *Beckett Baseball Card Monthly* and the annual *Official Price Guide to Baseball Cards*.

At the National Sports Collectors Convention in 1980, Dr. Beckett received the first "Special Achievement Award for Contributions to the Hobby."

While not ignoring the popularity of card investing, Dr. Beckett emphasizes the hobby aspects of collecting. He has assembled one of the finest collections, in both quantity and quality, of baseball and other sports cards.

"I started as a youngster. In fact my Dad collected and it was a natural thing for me to follow. I started when I was seven years old and pretty seriously collected until I was about 12. Then I withdrew from the hobby while I was in junior high school, high school and college. But I got back into it when I was in graduate school.

"I just love baseball. I played some baseball until I was 12 or 13 and then I started playing tennis. Then after I got out of college I started playing baseball and softball again. I've always followed baseball closely. That's probably one of the secrets of collecting—if you don't love baseball it's kind of hard to have a lot of staying power in a hobby that is centered on the game itself.

"Another secret is that when I was growing up I didn't get burned out with the cards. When I was a kid I wasn't allowed to look at the cards unless it was a rainy day or there was too much snow to go outside. If it was a nice day, I was outside playing baseball. If it was a bad day, I was inside looking at the cards.

"Even now I pace myself and get a lot of enjoyment from the cards.

"Unless you're bitten by the bug and start thinking that baseball is a pretty great sport that's had a great history, then you probably won't be in the hobby very long. The investment aspect is usually not sufficient to hold a person's interest for a long period of time."

As with postage stamps and rare coins, there are many different ways to approach the collecting of baseball cards. Dr. Beckett believes there is no single "right" way to begin with baseball cards.

"Go for what you like. It depends on the person's objectives. If you just want a hobby, obviously just go for what you like. If the objective is to have a hobby with some investment overtones, then maybe you should study the subject. I also believe in a trade off between specialization and diversification. If you're investing in the stock market and you could consistently pick the stocks that only go up, you wouldn't need to buy a mutual fund that contains some good stocks and some bad ones in it.

"It's the same thing with baseball cards. You can't go too wrong if you buy the whole set for a given year. On the other hand, typically the spectacular increases are going to come from the one player who goes from nothing to something all of a sudden. If you bought Eric Davis (of the Cincinnati Reds) or Roger Clemens (of the Boston Red Sox) when they first entered the majors you would be sitting pretty today.

"It is supply and demand. After the supply is produced it is a question of who wants what, and how the demand is affected by what happens on and off the field.

"Take the strange example of Wally Joyner (of the California Angels). There was a lot of demand for his cards even before they existed. People were waiting in line for them. He had a strong Winter League season in 1985-86, but none of the major card companies had him in their regular sets. He caught them by surprise, and collectors were really chomping at the bit to get his cards in the updated sets in the Fall of '86."

The annual *Official Price Guide to Baseball Cards* contains more than 400 pages of average retail prices for tens of thousands of different cards since 1948. His magazine tracks monthly price changes for thousands of cards. Even as a professional statistician, is Dr. Beckett sometimes amazed at the numbers involved in all those cards and all those price movements?

"I can't say they overwhelm me or I wouldn't be able to put out all the information that I do," he laughed. "I can say that it is very difficult. I am glad I'm a Ph.D. statistician or it would be near impossible. It's really pretty awesome. I don't claim to be perfect, but I do the best I can."

As mentioned earlier, Dr. Beckett believes the large number of different cards produced each year forces collectors to realize they not only can't collect one of every card ever made, they'll have trouble just trying to get one of every card made this year.

"That's good because it causes people to think, 'Hey, I'm not going to buy stuff just for the sake of buying something. What do I really want? What are my objectives?'

"The objective of having one of each card produced in a given year, whether it costs $2,000 or $5,000 or $7,000, generally is out of reach for the vast majority of collectors—both kids and adults.

"I think that's good. There's the survival of the fittest and the card companies that put out the best cards are successful. The most attractive cards are successful and the others fall by the wayside. The natural selection is good.

"Are there too many new cards being issued? There evidently aren't too many if people keep coming out with them and they're somehow being absorbed [in the marketplace]. Philosophically, sure there are too many; but economically, it's a free world. These companies [such as Quaker Oats] are paying for the rights to put out baseball cards for promotions with Chewey Granola Bars because they think it will enhance the sales of their products. It's a compliment to the hobby [that so many businesses are promoting cards]. It is indicative of the strength of the hobby.

"If people become bored and say, 'Aw, here's another baseball card—who cares?' then these companies would not issue more. They just wouldn't do it. That would be the way the marketplace would say there are too many cards being issued. But the marketplace apparently doesn't feel there are too many because collectors are swooping down and jumping all over these new issues, for the most part. There are an awful lot of collectors out there."

One of the regular features of *Beckett's Baseball Card Monthly* is the "Weather Report" section, a listing of readers' sentiments about the players who are hot and those who are not. It is a quick way to help determine the short-term potential for some players' cards to increase or decrease in value. As with several major hobby publications, Dr. Beckett and his staff devote considerable space to readers' letters and comments. From these letters and firsthand experience at conventions, weekend shows, and conversations with collectors and dealers, Dr. Beckett carefully monitors hobby trends.

"One of the major trends now is all the interest in the newest and the latest and the greatest players. For example, everybody is buying Dwight Gooden cards and believing that in 20 years he will be really valuable (an example of this popular card is on the front cover of this book). I just think that collectors should be history students, too, and realize that 20 years ago there was a guy named Bob Gibson with the St. Louis Cardinals. Back in 1968 Gibson had about the best E.R.A. of any modern era pitcher. Yet, his card today is worth only a few bucks; not much more than Dwight Gooden's rookie year card. Collectors must realize that for the hobby to continue thriving and be successful there has to be a marriage between the past and the present.

"If collectors in the 1980s don't put enough emphasis on the older players, then in 20 years when Gooden has retired and is only a great memory, there may not be much interest in his cards. There has to be interest in today's superstars after they've retired. That's the only thing that bothers me about the hobby.

"I encourage people to broaden their interests. Obviously, collect whatever you like, but I think it is bad to be so obsessed with the present that you forget the past. You can concentrate on the present, but try to broaden your interest to at least include something from the players of the past.

"And, if you want to help ensure that the card you're buying today will increase in value in the years ahead, you have to help promote the hobby. Encourage your friends to become collectors and participate."

Some hobby veterans worry that too much emphasis is placed on trying to make a quick buck instead of establishing a long term commitment to the hobby. Does Dr. Beckett agree?

"Again, the marketplace eventually is going to weed out those people if they only try to make a quick buck. Frankly, the marketplace is not going to weed them out now because it is real easy to make a quick buck with more people coming into the hobby and with the increased demand for more cards it is pretty easy for people to make money—either as dealers or collectors on a short term basis.

"But the long term future of the hobby is not based on short term buying and selling. It's based on a hobby that includes the enjoyment of the cards as well as any price increases. It is the enjoyment you have of owning, buying, selling and trading activities.

"You can't make a quick buck if the prices are only going up one percent a year. Some cards have gone up one percent or more a month, and then you have an opportunity to make money. Just like in the stock market if you buy a stock at $10 and it goes to $15, whether that happened in a month or in a year, you have an opportunity to sell. So the quick buck is determined not so much by the person, but by the price movement of the cards.

"We're in a period of very high growth in the hobby, and as long as that continues there are going to be those opportunities to take those profits.

"Philosophically, there's probably too much emphasis on the investment angle, but pragmatically speaking—economically, practically speaking—it's determined by the marketplace. There's no quick buck to be made unless there's a perceived scarcity or a demand that is greater than the supply.

"The primary thing is enjoyment of the cards. The investment can be an additional bonus. If you made $10, $100 or $1,000 in profit in a year you still have to factor in the enjoyment that you had with the cards—the kind of fun you generally don't have with a bland certificate of deposit.

"If you spent ten hours enjoying your baseball cards during a given month, and most people spend far more time, that time has a value to it. A positive, recreational value. Most collectors probably would tell you they'd rather spend time with their cards than go to a movie.

"If cards did not even go up in value you would still have collectors; maybe not as many, but you'd still have collectors.

"It is like buying a fine painting. There is a pride of ownership. If it goes up in value, that's great. On the other hand, even if it doesn't you still have the enjoyment of the painting. But then again people usually don't take a painting down off the wall and read the back of it, or trade their paintings with other owners of paintings.

"All these things that make the hobby great and have been responsible for its growth add up to one point: This is an enjoyable hobby!

"It is a great testimony to the hobby that there is so much strong word-of-mouth about the enjoyment.

"If you've got more kids in your neighborhood or more father and son teams in your Scout troop that have a collecting interest it will add to your own enjoyment and help keep the hobby thriving. There is a fantastic father-son, mother-daughter, family-oriented and team kind of aspect to the hobby. It is a positive experience, a wholesome, dynamic and exciting life-time hobby.

"Even if the prices were not going up like they have been, it would still be a lot of fun. The fact that cards have been a great investment the past five or ten years is a tremendous, extra bonus," Dr. Beckett emphasizes.

Another Heavy Hitter

An

interview

with Bob

Lemke

B ob Lemke not only collects baseball cards, he constantly reads and writes many articles about them. It is his job. Lemke is publisher of *Sports Collectors Digest*, a thick, every-other-week magazine loaded with valuable information about the hobby. He also is editor-publisher of *Baseball Cards,* a monthly magazine containing a price guide for thousands of cards issued since 1948.

"It's not real hard to get people started collecting baseball cards," he says. "It's sometimes hard to keep them active and get them to expand their horizons beyond what is currently available [the newly-released cards each year].

"Perhaps you've initially got to appeal to the 'Greed Factor' [buyers purchase cards in the hopes that they eventually will be able to sell them for a profit].

"Baseball cards are interesting because unlike most other collectibles they are directly related to things that are happening every day for half the year—baseball games. There is a direct correlation between a player's performance and the demand for, and value of, his baseball card. It is a situation that you just don't have in most other hobbies. Relatively new cards can quickly go up in value.

"It creates the liveliness in the hobby that we're getting while coins, stamps and a lot of other collectibles remain just static. As long as we can keep people interested in baseball as a sport the baseball card hobby should continue to do something."

Lemke urges collectors to purchase all the available rookies cards as soon as they are issued. He points to what happened to Dwight Gooden's rookie year cards. They quickly shot up in value after being issued late in the 1984 season.

Lemke believes that rookie cards, if purchased immediately after issue, are a small-cost investment with tremendous potential for profits.

"Certainly the best way to make sure you don't miss anything is to buy a complete set of cards right off the bat. It is not the most fun way to collect, but purchasing a complete set is the cheapest way [to get all the cards issued].

"By the first of the year the sports collectors' publications are filled with advertisements offering complete sets of that year's cards, and with so many dealers offering them at one time the sets are usually very competitively priced.

"While it is traditional to go to the corner store and buy one or two packs of cards at a time and then trade with friends to build an entire set, it is very repetitive because of all the duplicates you wind up with. And unless you're only getting duplicates of Don Mattingly and Dwight Gooden, it is not going to be financially beneficial.

"Once you've purchased a complete set and you're assured that you have not missed a great card that might become very popular a year or two from now, you've got the rest of the year to stay interested and active in the hobby."

As one of the "insiders" of the baseball card hobby and industry, Bob Lemke offers these tips for inexpensively acquiring potentially valuable cards.

1. THE SECRET OF THE CELLOPHANE PACKS

With a little bit of detective work and the cooperation of other collectors who live in your area, you can discover what cards are usually in the cellophane packs. "You can tell where to find the hidden from view Dwight Gooden or Jose Canseco or any other 'hot' cards by looking at the visible front and back cards wrapped in the cellophane package," says Lemke.

"The cards usually are printed, cut, and packaged in an almost perfect sequence. In the cellophane packs with 28 cards and a stick of gum there will be two sections of cards. Fourteen cards are above the stick of gum and 14 below. With a reasonable degree of certainty, particular cards are always packaged together and the order never varies.

"For example, in 1986 if you found on the top of the pack the cards of Ken Landreaux, Frank Viola, or Dave Kingman, then the next card after Kingman was almost always going to be Dwight Gooden. Similarly, there were certain press runs or sequences that usually contained Pete Rose, and so on.

"But to find that information about what cards are in predictable sequences you've got to go through some amount of packs to find what you're looking for. That's where having friends doing the same thing helps. You develop a network of friends who make a note of what other cards were packaged with the Gooden, Canseco, Rose or whatever popular cards you're looking for.

"Among the 14 cards above or below the stick of gum, the Rose card might be the second from the top, or the fifth, or some other location in the stack. But it should always be included together with the 27 other cards in a particular sequence.

"Once you know what those 27 other cards are you can then tell which cellophane packs have the particular card you're seeking. If you see one of the 27 others at the front, and another at the back of the package, chances are very good you'll find the Gooden or Rose card also in the stack."

Lemke says this is "a little-known secret" about baseball cards. Unfortunately, some of the people who know the secret are dealers who sell baseball cards. Some of the retail dealers, knowing what good cards are hidden among the stacks in the cellophane packages, take out the good packs and let their customers only buy the less desirable packages.

"We get a lot of complaints about that kind of thing from readers of our publications," Lemke admitted.

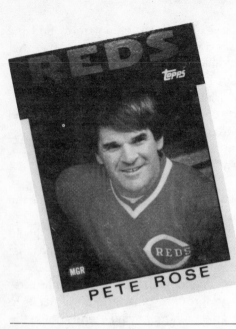

One of the most popular players of the past few decades, Pete Rose of Cincinnati as he appears on his 1986 Topps "manager" card (#741).

(James A. Simek Photo. Copyright Topps Chewing Gum, Inc.)

2. THE SECRET OF KNOWLEDGE

Lemke heartily agrees with the old expression that "knowledge is power."

"I guess the real secret about cheaply buying cards that could become valuable some day is to develop your own knowledge of baseball and be able to spot a player before he becomes the hottest thing around.

"You can do it on a widespread basis by following all the teams and all the players, or you can be more selective. You can follow your hometown major league team, or follow its farm club, and see who shows some potential. Watch in September when the top prospects are brought up for the month to get an idea if they have what it really takes. They could be next Spring's rookies.

"There's no substitute for good baseball knowledge in trying to anticipate the baseball card market.

"The same goes for players who may have been around the leagues for several years but are just now starting to show some potential. Ryne Sandberg cards were not really worth much until 1985 and his cards were three years old by then. If you had waited

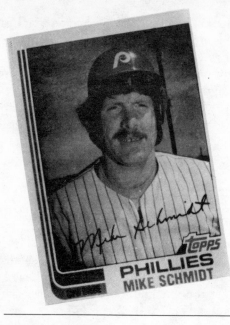

A long wait, but
worth it, for Mike
Schmidt's card to
increase in value.
The Phillies star is
shown here on his
1982 Topps card
(#100).

(Krause Publications Photo.
Copyright Topps Chewing
Gum, Inc.)

for Mike Schmidt cards to become valuable you'd have waited a long time.

"So you've got to develop knowledge about players and their potential abilities."

3. The Secret of Being Selective

Each year, thousands of different baseball cards are produced. Just among the "big three" producers of Topps, Fleer and Donruss, more than 2,300 different cards were printed in 1986. Plus, numerous other companies offer cards across the country as promotional items or as limited sets in specific regions of the country.

"If your goal is to collect one of everything that is coming out every year, there are just too many cards today," warns Lemke.

"It has become a financial impossibility for virtually everybody. There are logistical problems involved, too, because there are so many regional and local issues being produced that you've got to spend a lot of money to acquire them.

"The new collector must determine just what he wants the basis of his collection to be. Do you want one of everything that has been printed this year? That is an ideal situation because no matter which of those cards becomes valuable, you have it.

"But so much of the stuff on the market today remains worthless for a long time because of overproduction and things like that. We're getting a situation now where all these specialty sets coming out seem to feature the exact same two or three dozen star players. It is obviously intended to increase the sales of the products because you'll sell more superstars than a player who is batting only .210.

"The method I use is to perhaps buy a specialty set when it comes out if it happens to contain a specific player I happen to collect. If it doesn't contain it, then I don't buy the set because you really just can't buy everything any more.

"And you have to be selective about the price as well. It seems that when a new issue first becomes available, those who have it are going to push the price to the maximum. They are gambling that hoards will be available at the end of the year and prices may plunge downward. (The manufacturers try to get rid of leftover quantities and slash prices.)

"We saw that with the K-Mart card sets in 1982. When they first came out they cost $2, but within a few months the K-Mart stores were selling them for only a dime a set because there were just too many sets produced. Collectors who bought them for $2 are going to be waiting a long time to get back that $2," Lemke predicted.

Well then, with so many thousands of baseball cards being issued by dozens of companies, should collectors concentrate only on putting together sets based on the products of Topps, Donruss, Fleer or Sportflics? Veteran collector Lemke says, "No, not necessarily."

He urges you to assemble a collection based on a long-range goal.

"Maybe the basis is trying to get all your favorite players or your favorite team. Team collecting is very popular. If you do that you may have to buy a regional set over the course of the year. In 1986, there were three different sets available in the Texas area for the Houston Astros. A bakery, a soft drink company and a beer company produced team sets of the Astros in addition to the cards available around the rest of the country.

"These regional cards sometimes are made available to spectators on baseball card days at the stadium. There are very few teams that don't have somebody producing a regional card set of one kind or another now.

"So if you concentrated only on the three major card companies you're going to miss some very attractive, collectible cards. Often the producers of these regional sets are not concerned about national marketing trends and over-researching themselves to death. They are producing an attractive set of cards that will be very collectible. For example, the cards made by Mother's Cookies," explains Lemke.

Grading Baseball Cards

"Unlike other collectible hobbies which have one fairly uniform set of grading standards, the baseball card hobby exists with nearly as many grading standards as there are collectors and dealers," warns Bob Lemke. "No one, whether dealer or collector, is required to conform to any standard."

"Individual card dealers and collectors differ in the strictness of their grading," agrees Dr. James Beckett. He points out that determining the condition of a baseball card is very subjective.

Some guidelines do exist, and if rare coin dealers continue to enter the baseball card marketplace and exert their influence, grading standards probably will become more standardized—and stricter. For example, for generations dealers and collectors usually described a coin not exhibiting any signs of wear as "uncirculated." If a really nice specimen were offered for sale, it might merit the additional adjective, "choice." But in the past two decades there have been tremendous changes in coin grading—both good and bad—that possibly could happen to the grading of baseball cards.

The "uncirculated" category first was divided into three segments: average uncirculated, select uncirculated, and choice uncirculated. These are often given on a numerical scale as mint state-60, mint state-63, and mint state-65. As more investors moved into the marketplace, and a scramble to find the highest quality coins followed, some pieces that had been marked "only" MS-63 were suddenly being sold as MS-65 specimens. But when the boom market began to cool off in late 1980 and 1981 dealers' eyesight greatly improved.

Currently, there are 11 (count 'em, eleven) different designations of grade just in the uncirculated category, MS-60, 61, 62, 63, 64, 65, 66, 67, 68, 69 and 70. The adjective "gem" is frequently used, and now and then you'll encounter a "perfect" specimen, probably with a perfectly outrageous price tag accompanying it.

Isn't all this confusing? Yes.

Are all these designations necessary? That's debatable. It depends on who you ask.

"Precision grading" is a fact of life now in coins and to some extent in stamp collecting-investing. It is *precisely* what will happen in baseball card collecting if the pattern is repeated.

The multiple designations do not stop at mint state. Almost uncirculated (just a tiny trace of wear) and extremely fine (a little more wear and no original luster remaining on the coin's surface) have several divisions in their categories. While the price difference between a coin in extremely fine condition may not be much less than a similar item in almost uncirculated grade, there usually is a tremendous difference in price between a rare coin graded mint state-64 and a true mint state-65 piece.

Coin dealer Maurice Rosen accurately describes the effort to achieve precision grading as "the grading renaissance," but he also correctly notes that it has created a nightmare for many collectors, investors and dealers. Buyers who in good faith purchased "gem" quality items a few years ago have discovered that yesterday's "gem" may be only today's "choice" specimen—and with an appropriately lower value.

A generation ago, many postage stamp collectors affixed a hinge on the gummed back of most mint condition stamps so they could be mounted in an album. But today, stamps that have been hinged are worth less, sometimes much less, than comparable specimens accurately labeled "OG-NH," (original gum-never hinged).

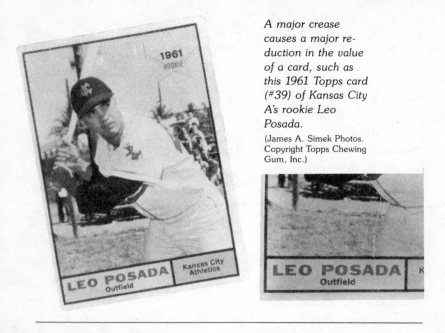

A major crease causes a major reduction in the value of a card, such as this 1961 Topps card (#39) of Kansas City A's rookie Leo Posada.

(James A. Simek Photos. Copyright Topps Chewing Gum, Inc.)

With stricter grading standards and increasing demand for only top quality items, baseball cards showing any stains from being packaged next to a stick of chewing gum or nestled against wax paper will be worth less than similar cards free of these detracting marks. And these mark-free cards must have edges and corners that are not coming apart in layers.

Only one category exists now to describe a baseball card showing no signs of wear: mint condition. With more and more grading-conscious coin dealers entering the card market and the increase in the number of investors, having just one category of "uncirculated" is grossly inadequate. Surely, a burst of adjectives will surface to describe better quality mint cards.

Choice, gem, superb, spectacular, dazzling, sharp, and even "wonder card" are some of the terms we'll be reading in hobby publications, price lists and auctions. And, of course, the better the adjective, the higher the price being asked for the card.

Already coin dealers' critical eyes are resulting in more demands for superb quality cards and tougher grading criteria. Tony Galovich of American Card Exchange in Newport Beach, California, is typical of card dealers eagerly ready to pay very high prices for many mint condition classics. Since 1985, one of his baseball card business partners has been David Hall of Irvine, California— one of the movers and shakers of the U.S. rare coin market and a major leader in the precision grading movement. Advertisements listing Galovich's prices carry the stipulation: "Strict grading essential to receive these prices. No off center or creased cards."

Galovich also makes a significant distinction in values between cards in excellent condition, those in near mint condition and those actually in mint condition. For example, one advertisement offered to purchase 1933 Goudy Babe Ruth cards for $260 in excellent, $410 in near mint and $675 in mint condition.

Remember, just a little difference in quality can mean a huge difference in price. The better the "eye appeal," the better the value of the card.

As the trend for more precise grading takes hold the faintest hint of a crease, the most subtle dents and nicks, the slightest out-of-alignment printing or the smallest trace of discoloration will lower the value of the cards. It might seem absurd now, but in the near future it may be common for many dealers to examine carefully higher-value cards under strong lighting with magnifying glasses, just as dealers and collectors now closely examine rare coins and postage stamps to determine their grades as well as authenticity.

And no matter how wonderfully a dealer may have praised the condition of the cards you were buying from him, the chances are good that those cards won't appear as wonderful to some other dealer when you try to sell them a few years later. That's a frequent complaint of stamp and coin collectors, and it's sure to carry over to card collecting.

Two major hobby publishers propose groundrules for determining the condition of cards. Here are the definitions used by Krause Publications, Inc. (*Sports Collectors Digest, Baseball Cards,* etc.) and Statabase, Inc. (*Beckett Baseball Card Monthly,* etc.). Notice the many similarities, yet the considerable room for different interpretations of the grading criteria.

This Lou Whitaker 1986 Topps (#20) is a card that would grade "Mint," but poor centering knocks it down to "Excellent" condition with a correspondingly lower value.

(James A. Simek Photo. Copyright Topps Chewing Gum, Inc.)

Krause

Mint (Mt.): A perfect card, well-centered with four sharp, square corners. No creases, edge dents, surface scratches, yellowing or fading regardless of age. No imperfectly printed card (out of register, badly cut) or card stained by contact with gum, wax or other substance can be considered truly mint.

Excellent to mint (Ex-MT): A nearly perfect card. May have one or two corners which are not perfectly sharp. May have minor printing imperfections. No creases or scruffiness on surface. May show hint of paper or ink aging.

Statabase

Mint (M or MT): A card with no defects. A card that has sharp corners, even borders, original gloss or shine on the surface, sharp focus of the picture, smooth edges, no signs of wear, and white borders.

(Categories between major condition grades are frequently used, such as very good to excellent (VG-E), fair to good (F-G), etc. The grades indicate a card with all qualities at least in the lower of the two categories.)

This 1961 Topps (#13) of Detroit's Chuck Cottier appears to be a "Mint" condition card, but the centering is off and a few corners are slightly rounded, lowering the card to "Excellent" grade.

(James A. Simek Photo. Copyright Topps Chewing Gum, Inc.)

KRAUSE

Excellent (Ex.): Corners and edges no longer sharp, though not markedly rounded or dented. Centering may be off, but all borders must show. No creases. Surfaces may show slight loss of original gloss from rubbing across other cards.

STATABASE

Excellent (E or EX): A card with very minor defects. Any of the following qualities would lower a card from mint to excellent: very slight rounding or layering at some of the corners, a very small loss of original gloss, minor wear on edges, slight unevenness of borders. These minor defects are so minimal as to be only visible on close inspection. In other words, an excellent card should look mint until you examine it closely.

This 1961 Topps (#27) of the Cubs' Jerry Kindall is an example of a "Very Good" condition card with some rounding of the corners and a light crease.

(James A. Simek Photos. Copyright Topps Chewing Gum, Inc.)

KRAUSE

Very good (VG): A card that shows obvious handling. Corners will be rounded and perhaps creased. One or two other minor creases may be visible. Surfaces will exhibit some loss of luster, but all printing is intact. May show moderate gum, wax or other packaging stains or defects. No major creases, tape marks, or extraneous markings or writing. Exhibits no damage, just honest handling.

STATABASE

Very good (VG): A card that has been handled but not abused. Some rounding at the corners, slight layering or scuffing, slight notchings on the edges. A very good card may have a very light crease if it is barely noticeable.

An example of a card in "Good" condition: Detroit outfielder Don Lund on his 1954 Bowman card (#87).

(James A. Simek Photo)

KRAUSE

Good (G): A card that shows excessive wear or abuse. May have thumb tack holes in or near margin, corners rounded into design, perhaps small tears. Will have one or more major creases breaking the paper, and several minor creases. May have minor added pen or pencil writing or other stains. Back may show evidence of having been taped or pasted, with small pieces of paper missing or covered.

STATABASE

Good (G): A well-handled card, rounded and layering at the corners, scuffing at the corners and minor scuffing at the face, notching at the edges.

This 1957 Topps card (#265) of Philadelphia's Harvey Haddix is an example of "notching," which significantly lowers the value of a card.

(James A. Simek Photo. Copyright Topps Chewing Gum, Inc.)

KRAUSE

Fair (F): A card that has been tortured to death. Corners or other area may be torn off. Card may have been trimmed, show holes from paper punch, or have been used for BB gun practice. Major portions of front or back printing may be missing from contact with heaven-only-knows what substance. Card may exhibit added decoration in the form of moustaches or writing in the form of derogatory comments on the player's ability, ethnic heritage or legitimacy.

STATABASE

Fair (F): Round and layering corners, brown and dirty borders, frayed edges, noticeable scuffing on the face. A heavily creased card can be classified as fair at best.

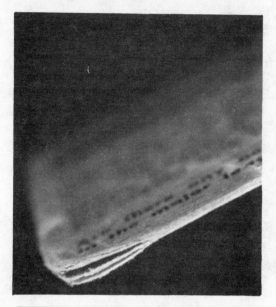

A severe case of "layering" where sections of the cardboard are coming apart—and the value of the card is lowered.
(James A. Simek Photo)

KRAUSE

(No proposed criteria for this grade.)

STATABASE

Poor (P): An abused card, the lowest grade of card, frequently some major physical alterations have been performed on the card. Collectible usually only as a fill-in until a better condition replacement can be obtained.

Cincinnati outfielder Gus Bell had a decent batting average, but this 1954 Bowman card (#124) is rated only "Poor" to "Fair" because of the rounded corners and many creases.
(James A. Simek Photo)

It usually is best to buy the finest quality cards you can afford. You may want to drive a Rolls Royce, Mercedes Benz, or Porsche, but if you can only afford a two-door Chevy then that's what you get. It is the same with cards. If you can't afford to purchase mint condition, then you happily purchase and enjoy something in a lower grade.

Just make sure that if you pay mint price you get a mint card, not one that grades excellent. And carefully examine cards labeled very good to determine if they really are. No matter what the price, buying overgraded cards will make you feel fair to poor.

Rookie Fever

High enough

to make some

collectors

delirious

The recent demand for the rookie year cards of some baseball players has been so hot it is a wonder the pieces of cardboard have not been singed. Unfortunately, in the long run some of the buyers of these cards may be the ones who get financially burned.

The editor-publisher of *Baseball Cards* magazine, Bob Lemke, describes the unprecedented interest in rookie cards as "the biggest thing to hit the baseball card hobby since bubblegum."

The rookie mania craze started around 1982. The three major card producers (and other card makers) vigorously compete with each other to be the first to issue cards with the hottest young players of the season. The collectors' requests for rookies even has sparked nationwide interest in "pre-rookie" cards, the sets of Minor League teams where "tomorrow's superstars" are first pictured.

In 1986, nearly 120 new American and National League players appeared for the first time on Donruss, Fleer and Topps regular and updated cards. Some rookies appeared on cards produced by all three companies; others were included by only one manufacturer.

So many different "Rookie Year" cards are available that *Beckett Baseball Card Monthly* uses different designations to separate them. A card listed by Beckett as "RC" (rookie card) is used to designate a player's first appearance on a regular issue card from Donruss, Fleer or Topps. It is considered *the* rookie year card or cards for that particular player (only one RC designation per player per company).

There are also designations for a rookie appearing the first time on an extended, updated, or traded set (XRC—extended rookie card), and if the Topps card of a particular player is issued after Donruss and Fleer have issued theirs (FTC—first Topps card).

The baseball card companies do not, for obvious reasons, include every Spring training rookie in the upcoming season's regular baseball card sets. The card manufacturers do carefully study the possibilities and select some young players with potential to appear in the initial printings released to the public at the beginning of each year. The manufacturers make additions, deletions, and other adjustments in the Fall when their updated and traded sets are issued.

The card makers not only must know how to print and distribute cards, they must know baseball and know it well.

"There's a lot of effort and knowledge of the players involved in coming up with rookies who may or may not have been considered for the following year," explains Fleer Corp. President Donald Peck. Even before the League Championship play-off games begin in early October, he and other card company executives begin selecting who will appear in the next year's series.

"We consider it, as our competitors do, a bit of a coup if we can come up with a player or two they haven't thought about putting into their regular sets. We've had a couple of winners that way which sparked sales nicely and filled the desires of the collectors who want something that may not be available in other manufacturer's series."

Topps spokesman Norman J. Liss points out that the baseball card "season" used to start with Spring training; however, now the company issues its regular, full card sets in January of each year. "In order to do that, we have to really make a lot of decisions before player trades are made, before some of the young ballplayers are on the rosters. So we issue a traded and updated series every September to include not only the players who were not in the regular series but also some players who now are wearing different uniforms."

Even with skill and luck the card companies for one reason or another may not have a superstar rookie in the regular season's series. It happened in 1984 with Dwight Gooden of the Mets. Both Fleer and Topps offered his cards (Fleer #43-U, Topps #42-T) in their year-ender extended sets.

Just what is the criteria used to officially designate a "rookie"? Lemke says:

"For a player to qualify as a rookie, he must not have achieved more than 130 at-bats or 50 innings pitched in the previous season or seasons. He also must not have been on the 25-man Major League roster for more than 45 days (in the previous season or seasons)."

Rookie players may be depicted individually ("solo") on the cards or in groups. From 1962 through the 1982 season, Topps produced rookie cards that usually featured two or more players on each card, often described as "multiple" rookie cards. For instance, Topps' 1981 card #302 shows three rookies of the Los Angeles Dodgers: Jack Perconte, Mike Scioscia and Fernando Valenzuela. At about $3 each in mint condition it is one of the highest valued cards of that year's set.

The 1977 Topps card #476 depicting four rookie catchers, Gary Alexander, Rick Cerone, Dale Murphy and Kevin Pasley, has rapidly increased in value the past few years to around $50 each in mint condition and is the highest priced item of that year's Topps regular set.

Earlier in this book you read about the interest in solo rookie cards with such players as Dwight Gooden, Wally Joyner, and Jose Canseco individually pictured. Some investors hope that these players' cards will have the same financial success as the 1963 Topps Pete Rose card (#537). Costing only a penny when it was first issued, the multiple player rookie Rose card has zoomed past the $500 mark in mint condition.

Fickle fans can quickly cool the temperature of "rookie fever." The value of Ron Kittle cards dropped when he went into a batting slump and was traded from the Chicago White Sox to the New

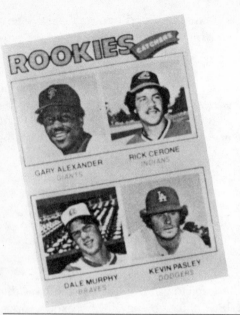

This 1977 Topps card (#476) depicting four rookie catchers has increased in value the past few years— it's also a quick way to collect a lot of rookies.

(Krause Publications Photo. Copyright Topps Chewing Gum, Inc.)

York Yankees. Many formerly hot prospects have turned cold either during their rookie year or after a few seasons. Conversely, a handful of players often catch fire after their rookie year, suddenly increasing the value of their cards.

To be informed about the potential of any player, you have to keep up with the game throughout the year, not just the season. That means reading the sports sections of the daily newspapers and closely reading *Baseball America, Baseball Digest, Inside Sports, Sports Illustrated* and other sports and baseball card hobby publications. The March issue of *Baseball Digest* annually rates the upcoming season's rookie players. Other magazines and newspapers contain specific articles about rookies and rookie cards and provide nuggets of information that can help you decide about players and their cards.

Some collectors and investors believe that as a Major League player becomes more popular—and his Major League cards increase in value—his Minor League cards should also go up in price. Recently that has happened. Enough interest has emerged across the country in Minor League cards to surprisingly kick up the price of traditionally cheap sets.

Why does the 1983 Lynchburg Mets card set sell for ten or more times its original issue price of $3? A young pitcher by the name of Dwight Gooden and a youthful shortstop named Len Dykstra happen to be included in that set.

Cal Ripken, Jr., can be found in the 1981 Rochester Red Wings; Wade Boggs' card is included in the set from the 1981 Pawtucket Red Sox; and in the 1982 Jackson Mets' card set you'll find Darryl Strawberry.

A total of 81 Minor League teams are included in recent card sets produced by Pro Card. Other companies producing Minor League cards are TCMA, Pacific Trading cards and Larry Fritsch. Some clubs issue their own team sets.

Some card dealerships, such as The Tenth Inning of Hampton, Virginia, refer to Minor League cards of Major League players as "the real rookie cards." They point out that Minor League card sets are produced in very limited quantities; usually less than 4,000 sets of each Minor League team are printed every year.

(To make collecting these cards much easier, The Tenth Inning has produced a "checklist" of more than 10,000 Minor League players and an inexpensive book picturing Minor League teams since 1972. For the current prices of these items write to: The Tenth Inning, 2211 West Mercury Blvd., Hampton, Va. 23666.)

Dealer Bill Wesslund of Portland Sports Card Co., Portland, Oregon, urges buyers to "get tomorrow's stars today" by purchasing the sets of Minor League teams. Dave's Sportscards of Pawtucket, Rhode Island (home of the Pawtucket Red Sox) proudly advertises that sets from the Minor League with "hot, pre-rookie cards. . . [are]. . . one of the hottest collectibles in the hobby." Minor league teams offer excellent investment potential if the current demand continues at the present pace or grows even bigger. That is, of course, a big "if." The possibility looms that future sets will be printed in much larger quantities to meet the growing demand; however, the sets already produced are in limited quantities.

Many other dealers buy and sell Minor League cards, either as sets or as individual cards. Sets can also be obtained at the souvenir stands in the Minor League ballparks (if that particular team has a card set).

If you're going to speculate on rookie players, either Major or Minor League, do not waste money purchasing anything less than mint condition specimens. The downside risk of losing a few dollars per set or card is not very big when you buy a current or recently-issued card, but the potential to make profit is much greater if the cards are in top quality condition. It is also easier to find potential buyers for high quality cards.

Remember, mint-only on current Major League rookies or Minor League sets unless you're buying something just to toss around on the sidewalk or carry in your back pocket.

If you are purchasing older rookie year cards, your finances will dictate the condition of the cards. If you cannot afford to spend about $150 for a mint 1955 Topps rookie Roberto Clemente (#164), then perhaps you'd be delighted to pay $50 or $60 for a very good condition specimen for your collection. Well-creased and worn cards are available for less than $15 each, but they can still make collectors proud owners.

Even though the potential for profits with rookie cards is tremendous, this area of the hobby must be considered speculative for now, like the "penny stocks" listed on the smaller stock exchanges. Most of the issues probably will go down in value. Now and then, however, a big winner can make up for the other losses and convince investors that speculation in rookie cards pays off well.

Rare coin dealer David Hall of Irvine, California (partner of Tony Galovich in American Card Exchange of Newport Beach, California) purchased 500 Don Mattingly rookie cards in 1984. He paid between $1.75 and $2.50 per card. Now those cards sell for five to ten times what he paid for them, depending on whether they are Fleer, Topps or Donruss issues.

Will the rookie mania continue?

Collector and sportswriter Paul Green does not think it is what card collecting really is all about.

"There's an awful lot of speculation at this point in modern rookies. People are having fun with it, almost like 'penny stocks.' I can understand it, although to me that is not what baseball card collecting is all about and it is not what I encourage people to do now. Cards are an interesting history of the game and the players and can be a lot of hours of pleasure, but I don't encourage people to speculate in $100 or $200 lots of Wally Joyner, Len Dykstra, or whoever is the hot property of the hour.

"In some respects I think there are too many cards today. I'm not really happy with the sheer numbers. First of all, I only need just so many pictures of any given player. It is a little frustrating to have so many. They are saturating the market. If people want to specialize in some of the lesser areas, fine. And it may be nice because collectors have an even greater selection to pick the pictures of the player they like the best," suggests Green.

"But I just couldn't possibly try to keep up with them all in terms of a collection. I certainly doubt that many people are doing it.

"Are some of these new issues overpriced? If someone wants to view baseball cards as an investment, then they can pay their money and take their chances on it. But this was not done when I was a kid. No one would hoard Mickey Mantle cards. Mickey Mantle cards were good trade bait, but that would be the only reason to have more than one of them. The object was to assemble a whole set. It was fun then, and it is good enough for me today.

"I know the minor league sets are hot, but those strike me as speculation more than anything. Sure, you can get the Madison Muskies team set with Jose Canseco's picture in it, but will this set really go up correspondingly with his unlimited career? Historically, the cards that have done well are the mainline rookie cards, especially Topps. And that assumes that Canseco or any other hot rookie is going to have a wonderful career. We've seen more than one example of players with brilliant starts that turned out to be rather deceptive compared to what actually happened during the rest of the career," warns Green.

"If you're in it for investment, you pay your money and take your chances. From a card collector's standpoint, I would basically be interested in players who made the major leagues. The minor league sets are interesting to some, but don't mean much to me other than in a vague sense. Others love them."

Green believes there is a valid argument to compare the craze for baseball rookies in the 1980s with the boom and bust of the numerous Franklin Mint collectors' items during the 1970s. At least when the market for Franklin Mint pieces collapsed, the silver medals still had some intrinsic bullion value. Pieces of cardboard do not have the same "safety net."

Dealer Kit Young of Vancouver, Washington, specializes in modern era baseball cards, but he warns collectors to avoid concentrating only on the new entries in the line up.

"This so-called rookie craze is great right now and kids can have a lot of fun with it, but over the long haul they'd be a lot happier with complete sets. In the sets they get both the hot players and the not-so-hot players," Young points out.

"There are stories about people who bought thousands of rookie cards of Mark 'The Bird' Fidrych, or Joe Charboneau, or Don Gullett, Dave Hostetler, Greg Brock and other players of the last few years. The buyers didn't like the results at all [the prices of the cards went up quickly and fell even faster].

"The players were supposed to be hot, but in most cases they were flashes in the pan," recalls Young.

Card Investments

"The market is in its infancy and prices are very cheap; therefore, long-term potential is spectacular," states veteran rare coin and now also baseball card investment advisor David Hall of Irvine, California. "Baseball card investing can be extremely profitable. A ground floor investment with spectacular upside potential," he emphasizes.

Hall is just one of the many coin and stamp dealers entering the baseball card marketplace. He brings to it many of the marketing and promotional procedures that have dominated numismatic (rare coins) and philatelic (postage stamps) trading since the 1960s. More of the established trends of coins and stamps are likely to become trends and patterns in the buying and selling of baseball cards.

Therefore, the three most important things to remember about successful baseball card investing are:

1. Condition
2. Condition
3. Condition

The condition, the grade of the cards, will be crucial in determining the value of the cards. As prices increase, buyers and sellers will make distinctions between "average" mint and "choice" or even "superb" mint condition cards. They will be priced accordingly, with substantial differences in value between the "average" cards and those that appear to have been centered with a micrometer, have surfaces as unblemished as fashion model Christie Brinkley's face, and have photographic colors rivaling the fireworks display at the Statue of Liberty's centennial celebration.

And when market "corrections" happen, when prices temporarily either stop rising or actually drop, the eyesight of these dealers will get even better. They will demand perfection in a card before paying top dollar for it.

Of course, other factors determine the value of baseball cards. They too should be considered when purchasing cards for investment potential.

1. SUPPLY

This is the first part of the familiar equation of "value = supply + demand." If there is a huge demand for an item, but not enough items to meet that demand, the price will increase. Conversely, if the demand falls far below the quantity available, the price will usually drop or at least stop climbing.

Even if the supply of cards is small, it does not automatically mean the value will be high; if plenty of cards are produced it does not mean their prices will be low.

If supply alone determined value, the prices for regional cards and Minor League issues would be very high; these cards are usually produced in limited quantities. It is the same with stamps and coins. Some "rare" items are valued at much less than items available in much greater numbers. The reason, of course, is that there is less demand for some issues and more demand for others.

2. DEMAND – BY COLLECTORS AND INVESTORS

"Our research has discovered that today's youngsters are very aware of the potential future value of their cards," says Topps spokesman Norman J. Liss. "When today's adults were young they'd stick a rubber band around the cards and shove them in a back pocket, then the cards would end up in a shoebox in the closet until mom threw them out. But now the kids are aware that today's rookies may be future stars and their cards may have potential value. So these cards are being placed in holders and carefully preserved in mint condition."

Liss points out that, at present, the greatest demand for cards comes from youngsters aged seven to twelve.

Hundreds of millions of cards are produced by the "Big Three" (Donruss, Fleer and Topps) each year, but does the huge quantity make a difference? Not while there is still an unbelievable demand for these cards. The modern cards are being purchased individually, in packages, by the full set, or even by the case (15 or more sets to a case).

There currently is a big demand for these millions of cards and an even bigger demand for specific cards such as the superstar rookies and the red hot veterans. That's why a Dwight Gooden card is valued higher than, say, the card of his teammate Mookie Wilson. Both have been good players, but Gooden is "hot."

If buyers are demanding certain cards, for whatever reasons, those cards probably will begin moving up in value, sometimes very quickly; week to week, day to day, and at card shows even hour to hour, price increases are common if the demand for specific items is high enough. A good way to discover what and who collectors are demanding is to read the major hobby publications, especially the "Letters to the Editor" sections, and to attend local and regional card shows where you can see firsthand what is being purchased by collectors.

3. DEMAND–BY MARKET MAKERS

Individual collectors and investors may purchase specific cards in quantities of one, a dozen or even a hundred. Major dealers often put out the word they are interested in purchasing hundreds and even thousands of modern era cards at a time. They become "market makers," establishing the wholesale (and eventually the retail) values of these cards.

No, you cannot quickly obtain a hundred mint condition 1952 Topps (#311) Mickey Mantle cards, but if several dealers begin raising their offers to purchase these cards the value of the few that might still be available will increase.

(Remember, those particular cards actually were printed in

"The" Mickey Mantle
card, the 1952 Topps
(#311) that com-
mands respect—and
big bucks—in any
condition.
(Krause Publications Photo.
Copyright Topps Chewing
Gum, Inc.)

double the quantity of most other cards in the 1952 Topps set. Even with a potentially larger number of the Mantle cards available, the demand is so high that mint specimens quickly sell for thousands of dollars each. That brings up another important subject, printing quantity. In the older series of the post-World War II era, the Topps cards with higher card numbers often were printed in smaller quantities than the cards with lower numbers. The higher numbered cards usually were printed late in the season and fewer of them were made. Some hobbyists debate whether all higher numbered-cards in those early sets merit a premium price over the more common lower-numbered cards.)

There are two easy ways to find out what the market makers are buying and what is in demand in the marketplace. First, read the "Want Ads." Dealers looking for specific items in large quantities often will place "Buy" advertisements in the major hobby publications indicating what they want to purchase. Frequently they will list their "buy prices" for various cards and sets in different grades. If the market is heating up for some items, the dealers' buying prices will be higher than the currently listed average selling prices in the major price guides.

The second way to be an "insider" is to attend major card shows. Just keep your eyes and ears open on the bourse floor, the merchandise area of the show where anywhere from a dozen to hundreds of dealers have tables set up to buy and sell. If you see several of the major dealers going from table to table trying to purchase large quantities of certain cards or sets the chances are good the values of those items will go up sometime in the future. It could happen that day, or it could happen a few weeks or months later when the purchasing dealer begins promoting the accumulated items. When that big retail promotion begins it's time to think about making your own profits by selling some of the same items from your collection, if you wish.

4. RARITY

As more research is conducted by collectors and dealers more knowledge is gained about the availability of some items. Cards previously considered "common" may be actually difficult to find in top condition. Cards that were hard to locate in high grade could suddenly drop in value when a large quantity of them are found in someone's attic or basement.

Many hoards of coins and stamps have been discovered and uncovered over the years. Often, when word of the find hits the marketplace, values of these items drop faster than a Fernando Valenzuela sinker. If the overall marketplace demand continues to increase the prices will eventually return to their previous level and even beyond it.

In the early 1970s literally hundreds of thousands of U.S. silver dollars were found hidden in the home of a reclusive Nevada millionaire. Some coin dealers predicted that the value of nearly all uncirculated silver dollars would drop because the marketplace could not absorb so many new items. But a few major dealers began promoting the sales of these coins and the U.S. silver dollar market zoomed upward.

In the early 1980s a hoard of several cases of 1951 Topps cards were found in Pennsylvania. Before the hoard was discovered, individual unopened packages were selling for $20 to $25 each. As the packages began to enter the marketplace the value dropped to less than $10 per pack. Chances are good that once that hoard is dispersed—and demand for the cards continues—the values will climb back up.

Sophisticated collectors who gain more knowledge and appreciation of early cards will realize that "classic" tobacco and early confectionery cards are rare in comparison to today's mass production issues. That appreciation of these earlier cards will be translated into higher values for them and for the already popular Bowman and early Topps cards that are "scarce" compared to today's production quantities but still available in large enough numbers to be actively bought and sold.

Among knowledgeable collectors virtually any cards depicting players in the Baseball Hall of Fame ("Hall of Famers") are desirable. Investors might want to speculate on those players who probably will be future inductees. Will the inexpensive 1954 Topps card #132, the only card showing Dodgers manager and former pitcher Tommy Lasorda as a player, jump in value when and if he becomes a Hall of Famer? What about the cheap 1961 Topps card #141 of former Cubs and A's star Billy Williams?

"Hall of Fame players tend to bring better prices," points out collector and hobby writer Paul Green. "When someone gets elected to the Hall of Fame his cards do not automatically jump. The cards tend to jump in price if the player has been selected by the Veterans Committee and it was a surprise choice. For example, catcher Rick Ferrell of the St. Louis Browns, Boston Red Sox, and Washington Senators played during the '30s and '40s, and for many people he just came out of the blue when the Veterans Committee nominated him to the Hall of Fame. He once had the unenviable task of having an entire pitching staff that only threw knuckle balls. At the time his salary was viewed as combat pay. He also was one of the first people to chart pitchers in terms of the number of pitches thrown and so on.

"Boston second baseman Bobby Doerr was another surprise to some people, but not to me. Ted Williams was named head of the Veterans Committee; he and Doerr were teammates!

"An awfully nice card collection would be composed of just the Hall of Famers. You would have a lot of cards covering a lot of years and it would be a good history lesson of both the game and baseball cards. It would not be something you could put together really cheaply because there are some $40 or $50 cards, even in used condition," explains Green.

Whether it is long-gone Hall of Fame veterans, rookie year cards, individual cards, or complete sets, the key to successful, long-term investment of baseball cards is the same as the traditional formula for investment in rare coins and stamps: Purchase high-quality items that have a history of proven demand.

5. QUALITY

High quality does not always mean mint condition. Some classic, early cards are virtually impossible to locate in mint condition. The same is true for many early postage stamps and coins; therefore, highest available condition is desirable even though it may be only very good (V.G.) for some extremely rare items.

As card collecting becomes more advanced we'll see increased use of such phrases as "finest known specimen," "top condition for its type" and "condition census." Depending on who is making the statement, you may need to take the information with more than just a grain of salt—sometimes an entire shaker.

"Finest known specimen" is an absolute statement. Are there really no other cards of this type in better condition? If it is a well-known classic, such as the famous Honus Wagner card, it is possible for dedicated researchers to track down the few dozen specimens that have been publicly offered for sale and make a comparison of their conditions.

When the quality of the best known specimens of a certain card, coin or stamp is known, researchers can establish a "condition census" listing of the finest three, four or five known examples. These individual specimens then have pedigrees, and they may become known by the names of the famous collectors who have owned them; for example, the Idler-Buss specimen 1804 silver dollar, so-named because its former owners included prominent 19th century Philadelphia coin dealer William Idler and Dr. Jerry Buss, a real estate developer and owner of the Los Angeles Lakers basketball team.

The phrase "top condition for its type," or something similar, is frequently used to indicate that while this particular specimen is not in perfect condition most known examples also are not. Sometimes it is an accurate description, other times it is used by dealers trying to unload large quantities of low-quality items.

When purchasing any card for investment purposes you must consider its quality in relation to its rarity as well as the potential for future demand. It certainly does not make sense to buy cards from the 1970s and 1980s that are not in mint condition. But purchasing the highest quality cards you can afford from the 1950s and earlier makes sense depending on your investment goals and finances.

If superb mint condition cards skyrocket in price, a big gap will open between them and cards in "only" excellent condition. Will the cards in excellent condition then move up in value, narrowing the gap to traditional levels? With stamps and coins those gaps were narrowed over time, but the highest quality specimens still command the highest values.

As a general rule, and in the collectibles market, rules can be made and broken faster than Billy Martin can run from the dugout. The value of many cards is based on what can be called the "10:5 ratio." A card in average mint condition is worth ten times more than the same card in fair to good condition, and five times more than in very good to excellent condition. As precise grading of cards increases, these ratios may change. It may become commonplace for a superb mint card to sell for three to five times more than an average mint specimen and even a hundred times more than the same card in very good condition.

One other important note on quality:

A card being offered for sale usually looks better to the seller than it does to the buyer. That's not a difference in eyesight, it is just human nature.

Big League Investing

The
strategy of
Alan Rosen

O ne of the country's largest card dealers, and a prominent figure at the National Sports Collectors conventions, is Alan Rosen of Montvale, New Jersey. His competitors may disagree with his comments about the market and his philosophy of baseball card investing and collecting, but the fact is: In recent years Rosen has done well over a million dollars in sales annually. He is known as "The Million Dollar Dealer."

Rosen points out that advertised "buy" and "sell" prices in most hobby publications are "already out of date" when the magazines hit the newsstands. It takes three to four weeks from the time the dealer places the ad until it appears in the publication. That may not seem like a long time, but in a market-place where card values change week-to-week and sometimes day-to-day, four weeks might as well be four years.

"For instance, mint condition Mickey Mantle cards. No matter what price you find in a book, the cards always bring more than the book value. It is the same with mint, pre-1975 sets of cards. They're always 30 percent

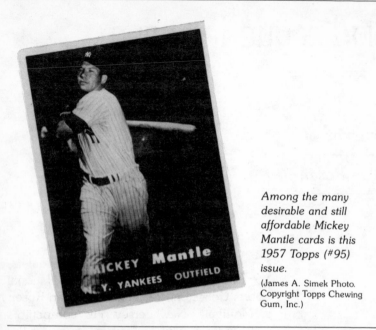

*Among the many
desirable and still
affordable Mickey
Mantle cards is this
1957 Topps (#95)
issue.*

(James A. Simek Photo.
Copyright Topps Chewing
Gum, Inc.)

higher than the book a month after the book comes out," explains
Rosen.

"It is not every card, but it is every Mantle and every nice condition early set. When *Sports Collectors Digest* listed a 1961 Topps
set at $950 and *Beckett Monthly* had it listed for $1,000 in its price
guide, I paid a thousand dollars for a set and immediately sold it to
a customer for 14-hundred."

When the coin and stamp markets are in a boom period,
dealers are involved in similar fast-paced buying and selling. Major
dealers will happily pay at least the "current retail prices" or even
more because the "current retail prices" as indicated by weekly
price guides are outdated. The dealers know the market and they
know other dealers or retail customers (collectors or investors) will
be delighted to pay a higher price for the materials.

During boom markets money is usually not a problem. The
problem is finding inventory, having enough items in stock for customers.

Because of the difficulty in locating adequate supplies of older cards and the sudden increase of so many collectors in the field, Rosen has joined other dealers in branching out into the buying and selling of sets and even entire, unopened cases of new issue baseball cards.

Rosen describes the rookie cards of Don Mattingly and Wade Boggs as "blue chip stocks. I try to stay with the popular, sure things. But I stay away from pitchers. Their next pitch could be their last. The cards of pitchers have not fared as well over the years as home run hitters," he says.

Two recent examples of pitchers' cards that have quickly gone up in value and dropped even faster are Rick Sutcliffe of the Chicago Cubs and Bret Saberhagen of the Kansas City Royals.

"Someone like Don Mattingly is a proven player. He's hit .330, .340, he's hit .350. I don't mind diving into the market with someone like that. I stay away from the 'hot' rookies," Rosen stated.

Earlier in this book, a half-dozen dealers and collectors recommended purchase of entire card sets each year. Rosen agrees. In fact, Rosen was suggesting it before many other dealers agreed with him. Rosen thinks investors should purchase entire cases of current card sets at $200 to $300 per case depending on the manufacturer and the type of sets (wax pack or vending packages) enclosed in the case.

"Cases, I think, are the best investments in the hobby right now. Let's say that in 1987 you decided to buy five of the 30 to 50 new rookies cards that came out at the beginning of the year. You think those five are good and you buy a thousand of each of their cards.

"What happens if each of the five zonks out? What happens if they're not good players? What have you got? You have nothing.

"But if you purchased an entire 1987 Topps set, then you've got one of everybody. If one of the rookies is not good, there will be another player who goes up."

Rosen describes this kind of full-set purchasing as an annuity. "Anytime a guy gets hot your set goes up in value. You can't lose."

Some speculators are purchasing unopened, "factory sealed" cases of cards, perhaps not understanding or even knowing for sure what is inside them. They only think of the cards as stock certificates, purchased today at one price to be sold tomorrow, they hope, for more money.

During the last rare coin boom, some "investors" purchased sealed tubes of silver dollars not knowing the exact date, mintmark and condition of each coin inside. Sometimes the buyers made a profit reselling the rolls of coins, sometimes they did not. It may be the same in the future for investors who hoard unopened cases of baseball cards hoping that more speculators will enter the marketplace and purchase more cases and sets.

The 1986 Topps regular set contains 792 cards (not including the extended set or mini cards or other special items). Both Fleer and Donruss have 660 cards in their regular sets. Depending on what brand you buy and whether the case contains wax packs, cello boxes, vending boxes, or whatever, each case will contain between 15 and 30 card sets.

If you purchased a case of 1986 Donruss vending cards you'd get 15 complete sets. That's 9,900 cards! Fifteeen sets of Topps 1986 cards amount to 11,880 cards. Not exactly a small "collection" that can be conveniently housed in a desk drawer.

As long as the market for cases and sets remains hot, or even a little warm, tremendous profits will be made on the buying and selling of these items. Yet the pattern of the coin and stamp markets indicates that eventually collectors and investors will concentrate on "classic" items. Not necessarily very scarce items—these, too, will be in demand—but individual items that symbolize some history, art, and romance—and potential for profit.

Although lots of attention is focused now on new issues from the major manufacturers, lots of money is available for purchasing earlier Bowman and Topps sets—when they can be found in mint condition. Rosen says many buyers want those sets from the early 1950s. There are buyers, too, for nice cards from the 1930s and '40s, but not nearly as many as those who want "the classics" issued in the decade after World War II.

Putting together an entire set of these cards is easier than trying to piece together entire sets of pre-World War II cards. Few people try to put together entire sets of Goudy cards—it is difficult and expensive to locate all the cards in nice condition. (Former player and well-known NBC sportscaster Joe Garagiola is an avid collector who proudly has assembled complete baseball card sets dating back to the 1920s and has many earlier cards in his collection.)

Rosen says he would buy an "unlimited" amount of nice Goudy cards, but he believes the Bowman and the 1952-1957 Topps cards would move faster in the current marketplace.

Gems or Junk?

A quick lesson in baseball card buying is posted on the countertop of a neighborhood printer's shop in a Chicago suburb. Aware of his competition's printing fees, this merchant's small sign reads: "The bitterness of poor quality remains long after the sweetness of low price is forgotten."

This axiom is applicable to nearly all phases of merchandising, not just cards. Many times you can find a bargain, but usually you have to pay the price for quality. If you go card shopping looking only for the lowest cost you still could end up "paying a price" by not getting the quality you sought.

As card collecting rapidly expands more collectors will make purchases through the mail from dealers across the country. The majority of these mail-order dealers will be honest merchants who want to sell accurately described and graded merchandise at fair prices; after all, they want to stay in business by making repeat sales to their customers— and to the friends of their customers.

Some dealers, however, will consistently lure customers with advertised "wholesale" prices for top quality material and fail to make good on their grading claims. The choice quality mint card may be only average mint, or worse, only in excellent condition.

The controversy over grading of baseball cards is nothing new to hobby collectors. Over the past few decades stamp collectors and dealers have complained about the differences between the grades of mint fine and mint very fine, if there is original (OG) gum on the back of the stamp, and so on. Numismatic researchers Dr. Richard Bagg and James J. Jelinski traced the problems of rare coin grading back to 1892.

Unfortunately, baseball card grading has no universal standards. Much subjectivity is involved in assigning grades even when an opinion is based on one of the grading guides found in popular hobby publications.

The final score for any buyer, whether purchasing just one card that is only fair or an entire mint set, is to get proper value for the money.

Ask yourself: If one dealer is advertising to buy a particular mint condition card for $300, why would another dealer want to sell one for $150 or less? There are a few answers. Perhaps it is an old ad, and the selling price is very outdated and should be much higher than $150. Or the $150 card is really not mint condition.

Or perhaps here at last is the world's only rare card merchant actually in business only for health reasons, not interested in making a normal profit of any kind. That indeed would be a rare card dealer—a rare dealer of any kind.

No one, but no one, will knowingly sell quantities of highly sought-after, top-quality material at below wholesale costs through normal retail channels.

There are no "fire sales" or "inventory clearances" when it comes to the top quality cards of the super stars. Be suspicious of any such offerings involving hot current or former players. Be suspicious of people who offer to sell only mint condition cards at unbelievably low prices but only seem to buy large quantities of lesser quality items.

The Better Business Bureau has a wonderful motto: "If it seems too good to be true, it probably is."

To slightly alter the warning of former coin collecting hobby publisher Lee Hewitt, "there is no Santa Claus in baseball cards."

So, what do you do? Feel dejected and scratch your name from the baseball card collecting lineup? No, just become knowledgeable about the game of baseball. You should also become a knowledgeable and responsible customer. Here are some common sense recommendations for astute mail-order buying.

In medium and large-sized display advertisements in Krause Publications hobby periodicals (*Sports Collectors Digest, Baseball Cards* magazine, *Baseball Card News,* etc.) look for Krause's Customer Service Award logo. It indicates that the advertiser has established a good track record in dealing with customers and promptly correcting mistakes or resolving complaints.

When regional and national card clubs or associations are formed or professional dealers organizations are established, look for the club or organization's logo or affiliation in a dealer's advertisement.

Small-sized ads may not have room for the logo or other references to membership in such groups, so do not eliminate a dealer from consideration solely because the logo is not present in the advertisement. Dealer membership in various organizations is not a blanket endorsement, but it does emphasize apparent concern for being in the mainstream of the hobby and a sign of commitment by the dealer to supporting worthwhile groups.

All reputable mail-order dealers provide return privileges. When your merchandise arrives examine it immediately. Did it come damaged? Is it what you ordered? Can you determine the grade? If not, show the cards to someone you believe is knowledgeable, perhaps a local dealer or other collectors in your community.

(A local card shop owner may not be happy about a stranger asking for advice about another dealer's merchandise. But if the shopowner has the time and the spirit of collecting fellowship he will want to educate new collectors and answer questions.)

If you are unsatisfied with the mail-order merchandise, for any reason, send it back by insured mail. If the purchase was large enough, say over $100, consider sending it both insured and registered mail and request a return receipt card.

If you are going to return any merchandise it must be done within the time limits set by the dealer or the publication carrying the advertisement. You can usually find that time limit under the "terms of sale" section of the ad. You usually have at least five days to inspect the items and get them back in the mail.

Honest mistakes do happen. Just because you ordered a card in excellent condition and it arrived looking more like Captain Kidd's long-buried and often-folded treasure map or a Billy Williams card arrives instead of Ted Williams does not mean the dealers are intentionally trying to cheat you.

They may have reached into the wrong storage box while filling your order. They may have left the house without breakfast that morning because their spouse and kids were yelling at them. They may have gotten your order mixed up with someone else's. Maybe they could not decipher your illegible handwriting.

If a mistake is made in the grade or type of merchandise you ordered, send it back with a brief, concise explanation of why you are returning it and politely request a replacement. Enclose a photocopy of the dealer's invoice and save the original for your records. If the cards are sealed in any kind of protective holders do not remove them.

If the replacement order you then receive is unsatisfactory (because of overgrading, for example), immediately send it back and demand a refund for both your purchase price and your postage costs. You might even send photocopies of your now indignant letter to the publishers of the newspapers or magazines normally carrying this dealer's advertising. The publishers should want to know what is happening since they probably want to protect their readers and protect honest advertisers from unfair competition.

They especially will act if they get enough unfriendly letters.

Be sure you always include your clearly-written or typed name and address on your order and on all correspondence.

List any second choice in case the items you order are sold out. Don't forget to include adequate postage if it is requested, and also add the applicable taxes, if any.

If you follow these few guidelines you should have no problems buying cards with confidence through the mail.

There are no formal requirements to become a baseball card dealer. Anyone can have an impressive business card printed or purchase prominent advertisements proclaiming himself or herself a dealer. The reality, though, is that many of the card dealers are

part-timers. They deal in cards as a side-line job. They travel to the
weekend shows or neighborhood flea markets and set up tables,
or they walk up and down the aisles at the shows buying and selling as a "vest pocket" dealer. (That's a popular although inaccurate
term indicating the dealer who carries his entire inventory in his
vest pocket.)

If you don't know your baseball cards then you'd better know
your dealer.

When you order through the mail, chances are the printed
price will be the price you pay for the merchandise. When you buy
at a card store or show you may be able to bargain with the dealer.
Most dealers would rather sell their merchandise and not "operate
a museum." If you want something but you feel the price is out of
line, ask, "Is that the best you can do?" Perhaps the price will be
reduced a little.

Before buying anything you should know the average retail
prices being quoted for similar items. That's where the latest hobby
price guides are helpful. Remember they are guides only, and
prices are not "etched in stone." Some dealers charge more, some
less, than what is quoted in price guides. Some dealers have
higher overhead costs or a dealer may have paid more to obtain
the desired items. Price is important in deciding whether or not to
buy, but price alone should not be the determining factor. A "high-
priced" dealer may be willing to spend quite a bit of time answering
your questions, making recommendations, and helping you locate
specific items for your collection. It is difficult to put a price on
those kinds of important factors.

When selling cards, especially more valuable items, you
should give the original seller an opportunity to purchase them
from you. If the merchandise is truly high-quality, most dealers
would be delighted to buy it back and offer it to another customer.
On the other hand, if you have to put together a very specialized
collection (i.e., early tobacco issues), you may want to sell it to
someone who specializes in this material. Or you may want to consign the items to an auction.

Some dealers may sell your collection piece-by-piece on consignment, taking a percentage of the total sale price per piece as
commission. Depending on market conditions and the salesman-
ship and clients of the dealer handling your consignment, it might

take a few hours or a few months to dispose of all the cards you want to sell.

When a dealer purchases your cards he may not be buying them for retail sales. The dealer may act as a middleman, selling your cards and others to dealers who will offer them to retail customers. If a dealer is acting as a middleman, you may get less for your cards than if you sold them directly to a dealer who has a ready retail customer for them. However, there are instances in which a smart middleman can offer you more for the cards because he or she knows exactly how much he or she can get for the items from certain dealers presently looking for that kind of material.

Again, if you don't know your cards you'd better know your dealer.

There are two more important points to remember when selling baseball cards. First, know the approximate value of your collection. Determine the grade of each card and its average retail price as indicated in current price guides. If it is rare, high-grade material, a dealer handling these kinds of cards may be able to offer you 10 to 25 percent less than retail value. If you believe the collection has a retail value of $10,000 you may be able to ask and receive anywhere from $7,500 to $9,000 for the items. If dealers and investors are scrambling to locate these cards you probably could ask $13,000 for the collection and some dealers would gladly write you a check. Whether you are buying or selling you should know the state of the current market.

If you have common cards in commonly available condition you may only receive 40 to 50 percent or less of current retail for the collection. An accumulation of 1,000 Bo Diaz cards may have a retail value of $50, but a dealer may only offer you $20 to $25 for them—if he even wants to buy them.

When you offer cards to a dealer be sure to quote a price. If you don't, the dealer may not want to even look at the cards. If you don't quote a price and he must "make an appraisal," he has to do the work without a guarantee that you'll accept his offer. Why should he make a good faith offer and have you reject it so you can take your cards to a competitor and ask for a few dollars more?

If you want a written appraisal of the wholesale or retail (replacement) value of your cards, dealers usually charge for this service based on the appraised value of the collection—usually about five percent or less. The appraisal fee then is usually waived if you promptly sell the cards to the dealer making the appraisal.

Second, if you are selling an entire set never let the buyer pick and choose only some cards from it. Sell the entire set. If a buyer "cherrypicks" the best cards from your set the value of the remaining cards will drop.

Fair or Foul?

Buying

and selling

at auction

Many baseball card buyers and sellers use auctions. There are many advantages, but there are some drawbacks.

Auction sales are a well-established way of life in the art world, and with rare stamps and rare coins. Catalogues describing and illustrating the items are produced and distributed to potential bidders. Usually a modest price is charged for the catalogues. Buyers and sellers from around the world attend major sales. Sometimes the bidding is hectic, with several buyers determined to own the same auction lot.

The major sales usually focus on high-grade or scarce items. If inexpensive items are offered they often are grouped together in lots rather than individually. Smaller auction events will provide buyers of more modest financial resources the opportunities to bid on less expensive items individually.

Another popular way to buy and sell at auctions is through mail bid sales. These sales usually appear as paid advertisements in hobby publications, and sometimes the auction company will mail to its customers a small catalogue or a reproduction of the advertisements. All the bids are made through the mail and must be received by a specific date. Bidders do not converge at a prearranged site. The winning bidders are notified by return mail and are sent invoices for their purchases. After they pay the invoices the merchandise is sent by the auction company.

More and more mail bid sales are appearing in baseball card publications. For decades, stamp and coin collectors have bought and sold items through these kinds of sales. Card collectors are now enjoying the benefits of this kind of leisurely yet exciting method of purchasing and selling cards. It is fun to read the auction lot lists, figure out how much you want to spend on each lot, submit bids, and eagerly wait for notification that you have successfully bought what you wanted—and at a price you wanted to pay.

Auctions are not only a convenient way for collectors and investors to obtain the items they desire, they are a convenient way for card owners to dispose of their holdings by consigning cards to auction companies.

But there are disadvantages. How accurate are the auction lot descriptions? Are the "mint condition" cards really mint or only excellent? Are the rare cards offered in the sale actually genuine, or cleverly deceptive reproductions that might fool someone without the expertise to spot a fake? Are the minimum bids established for some lots so high that you might be better off purchasing a similar item directly from a retail seller?

Are you sure you'll receive the money you anticipated for the cards you've consigned to be sold at the auction? What happens if the cards don't bring the prices you expected? How reputable is the auction dealer?

Here are some guidelines for easy buying and selling of cards at auction.

1. READ THE FINE PRINT.

Every auction sale has rules. If it is a mail bid sale, the publication carrying its advertisement may have rules that all auctioneers and bidders are obliged to follow. Auction sales catalogues usually have a page near the beginning of the sale outlining rules participants must follow for their bids to be considered.

If it is a mail bid sale, do you have the right to return merchandise that is not satisfactory? If so, under what circumstances and how quickly can you ask for and receive a refund? If it is a traditional auction in which bidders gather together for the sale, the bidders from the floor may not have the right to return lots unless they can prove items are not genuine.

Read and follow the rules carefully. They can save you money and embarrassment.

2. SET SPENDING LIMITS.

Carefully determine how much money you want to spend per lot. What is the lot really worth? How badly do you want the items? Many veteran bidders make notations in their catalogues to remind themselves of their bid limits per lot. During the heat of an auction these notations can prevent you from spending more than you intended for specific lots. After determining how much you'll bid per lot, add up all the proposed bids. Is the total amount more money than you are prepared to spend at one time? What happens then if all of your bids are successful and you receive an invoice for all those lots?

If you are not going to buy, then don't bid. Frivolous offers, for example bidding $10 on a card that easily will sell for $100, are quickly rejected by auctioneers. But if all your reasonable bids are successful you might spend more money than you previously planned. Some mail bid auction companies will let you set a monetary limit for expenditures. If you reach that prearranged spending limit you will be taken out of the auction at that point even though you may have submitted bids for additional lots.

A few auction dealers ask bidders if they want to increase their mail bids by 10, 20 or even 30 percent to be competitive with floor bidders at the sale. This is a tricky situation. How much do you really desire that auction item? If you make an initial bid that is liberal enough you should not have to worry about winning the lot. But are you prepared to pay a much higher price if others in the audience really want that same lot?

Suppose you send in a bid of $100 for an auction lot and it is the highest bid received by mail for that particular item. Suppose the highest floor bid for that item at the auction is only $50. Will the auctioneer declare your bid the winner and send you the lot with an invoice for $100, or will you be able to buy the item for less? Most reputable auction companies will sell you the item for a modest increase over the highest floor bid. In this case, perhaps $60. Some, however, will send you an invoice for the highest amount you submitted as a bid, in this example, $100.

Some auction houses charge a buyer's fee, an additional percentage added to the winning bid for each lot. If the buyer's fee is the traditional 10 percent, and you are the successful bidder of a lot at $50, your actual price will be $55. Keep the buyer's fee in mind when you are figuring out your bidding limits. If you are picking up your auction items at the sale, you'll have to pay the local sales taxes. If you're having the items shipped to you, you'll have to pay for the postage, registration and insurance costs. All these fees and costs must be considered when bidding.

3. CAREFULLY EXAMINE THE LOTS.

If you are attending the auction as a floor bidder, you must examine the lots before the sale gets underway. Auction dealers set up special viewing times, often by reservation for veteran clients, so that bidders can look at the items being offered in the sale. Many dealers will refuse to let winning bidders return merchandise (except for counterfeit items) if the lot was purchased in person. The assumption is made that a floor bidder has inspected all lots on which he or she is casting bids.

Experienced bidders often will jot down comments as they study the lots during a viewing session. You might note that this particular card has slightly faded colors in the corner, is well-centered, or is similar to another lot being offered elsewhere in the sale. These notes may prod the bidder to raise a bid, or even drop out of the bidding for certain lots.

4. PAY PROMPTLY.

If you have not established credit with the auctioneer, you may be required to pay for the lots before you can take possession of them. Some mail bid dealers will promptly ship the items to the winning bidders accompanied by the invoice for payment. Others want the money before they'll send the merchandise. Again, read the rules of the specific auction.

Auction dealers frequently exchange information with one another about customers who fail to pay promptly or who repeatedly return merchandise. These customers quickly find their future bids are ignored—across the country.

5. ARE YOU SATISFIED?

Did the merchandise you received match the description in the auction listing? Did the dealer promptly ship the items to you either immediately following the sale or immediately after receiving your payment for the items?

If you are pleased with your new possessions, you may have the start of a long, pleasant relationship with the auction house. If you are not pleased, let the dealer know why. Honest mistakes do happen and a reputable dealer will quickly try to resolve any problems. However, if repeated transactions with the dealer are less than pleasant, find another dealer. And let your friends know about your experiences, good and bad.

6. CAREFULLY CHOOSE THE AUCTION HOUSE
FOR CONSIGNING YOUR CARDS.

If you want to sell cards at auctions, you may want to consign them to one of the dealers from whom you have purchased cards over the years. If they are choice quality, scarce items the dealer should be delighted to offer them to other clients.

If you don't know about specific auction houses from personal experiences, talk with others in the hobby. What do they think about the specific dealers? Just because some dealers have received rave reviews, are they really the ones who should be handling your particular cards? Do you want to consign your 19th century tobacco cards to a dealer who specializes in modern, post World War II issues?

Will the dealer promote the upcoming auction to attract the greatest number of bidders? Are your cards insured while in the dealer's possession? If your consignment is substantial, will the dealer pay you a liberal cash advance based on a percentage of its estimated worth? Can you place a minimum bid or a reserve on the lots to protect your investments? If a card cost you $200, and you believe it should bring least $300, you don't want to see it sold at auction for only $150.

Most auction dealers will indicate any minimum bid levels or even reserves set for the items being offered in a sale. With a minimum bid, the bidding will start at that pre-determined level. If there is a reserve, the bidding may start at a lower point, but the auctioneer will have the right to withdraw the lot from the sale if the bidding stops before it gets to the reserve point.

Even if nothing is specifically indicated there are shrewd ways to boost prices. Bidders at the sale should be aware that the consignor might be bidding on his or her own items to "protect" his or her investments. Perhaps there may be a "shill" or some other accomplice in the audience who has no intention of buying that particular lot but is bidding only to increase the final price.

Just as with buying at auctions, there are rules for selling items at auction. Find out about them from the dealer.

Because of bookkeeping and other factors some auction houses have minimum consignment amounts. If the dealership specializes in fancy, colorful catalogs it may not want to accept for sale cards only fetching a few dollars each, or the cards might be sold as groups of several or dozens of cards per lot. On the other hand, if you have many valuable items you probably do not want them lumped together into one or two big lots; you want them individually presented in the auction sale with enticing descriptions of each of your prized possessions. Find out the policy of the auction house on how consignments are grouped for sale.

7. FIND OUT ABOUT FEES.

Some auction houses use a sliding scale of seller's fees charged to those who consign material for sale. If you have an estimated $500 worth of material, the dealer may charge you a fee of 20 percent of the winning bids for your cards. That fee pays for cataloging and listing your items, advertising, insurance and other expenses associated with conducting the auction. If you have many thousands of dollars worth of desirable items for consignment, dealers frequently will significantly reduce the seller's fee.

Some auction houses may give consigners a cash advance of perhaps 25 to 50 percent of the estimated value of their materials as soon as the dealer signs an auction contract with the consigners. If the dealer believes your merchandise will bring a combined total of $1,000, you may get an immediate check for $500. If the material does bring $1,000 at the auction, and your seller's fee was 20 percent of the winning bids (in this case $200), you would get a second check in the amount of $300 as your final payment.

Ask the dealer how quickly you can expect payment following the auction. The standard time period is 30 to 45 days after the end of the sale. That gives the auction house time to collect the money from the winning bidders.

Profitable Problems

S ome collectors of postage stamps and rare coins often will pay a considerable amount of money to purchase someone else's mistake. A common, misstruck one cent piece may be worth only a dollar or so, but other penny errors, such as a coin that was accidentally struck several times before being ejected from the minting press, may be worth a few hundred dollars.

A silver dollar from the late 1800s, struck so far off-center that a third of the coin's design is missing, can command a price tag of $1,000 or more.

The famous "inverted Jenny" U.S. 24-cent denomination airmail stamps that were accidentally printed with an upside down bi-plane always attract gawking spectators when specimens are placed on display. When one of those rare specimens is offered for sale thousands of dollars will change hands.

Even less spectacular stamp errors—significantly wrong colors, missing perforations (the series of holes along the sides of stamps that make it easy to tear the stamps apart)—usually make an otherwise common stamp much more valuable.

Coin collectors may pay big bucks for grossly mis-struck coins, such as this double-struck Eisenhower dollar, but most picky card dealers and investors would shun this otherwise valuable 1957 Topps Willie Mays card (#10) because it was printed so far off-center.

(James A. Simek Photos. Copyright Topps Chewing Gum, Inc.)

Interestingly, when it comes to baseball card mistakes the cards that do *not* contain the errors usually are worth more than the same cards *with* the mistakes. There are exceptions in which the error card has a much higher value than the corrected version. But usually the ones with misspelled names, incorrect statistical information or the wrong player's photo are not worth as much as a "good" card.

The last year Bowman issued its own set of cards, 1955, five cards were printed incorrectly (six if you count numbers 195-A and 195-B, the Erv Palica cards, printed with and without information about a player trade). In every case, each of the five error cards is worth considerably less than its corrected version.

The card (#48-B) showing Milt Bolling on his own card is valued at about $5; however, the card (#48-A) with Milt's name but Frank Bolling's picture usually sells for only about $1 in mint condition.

Two valuable error cards are in the classic 1952 Topps set. The statistics and other information about Joe Page were mistakenly printed on the back of the Johnny Sain card, and Sain's stats accidentally went on the back of Page's card. Apparently the errors were caught early enough so that the corrected version far out-numbers the errors.

Errors of fact can easily slip through even the most complete efforts to edit them out. Occasionally, mistakes occur in the check-list cards with players being listed with incorrect card numbers.

With so many facts and figures for so many different major league players surely some numbers are going to be placed in the wrong location or on the wrong player's card. Here are two recent examples:

Although he had only one stolen base the previous season, Kent Hrbek's 1985 Fleer Twins card (#281) mistakenly credits him with 14. That actually was teammate Kirby Puckett's total.

The 1984 Donruss card for Salome Barojas (#570) gives two different statistics for the pitcher's saves in 1982. The short biogra-phy of Barojas indicates he had 23 that year, but in the stats column on that same card it states he had 21. The correct figure is 21.

Neither of these two errors were corrected during the particu-lar year the cards were issued. These cards do not have any addi-tional value because of the mistakes.

Now and then a major printing error can become valuable, but usually minor changes in the color of printing ink, or a blob or streak of ink where it shouldn't be, do not add any value to the card. In fact, many collectors will not want to own it because it is not a "good" example of the card.

The 1983 Donruss cards of Ozzie Virgil (#606) have either the intended orange-colored frame around the card or a mistakenly printed green frame. Both the error and the corrected color ver-sions sell for virtually the same price.

There has been, however, a $10 value recently placed on the 1983 Donruss card of Ron Jackson (#639) that has a red border and shows the team's insignia as "A's" in Jackson's glove. Other ver-sions of the card with either a red or green border and the name "Angels" usually sell for less than a dollar.

"It's a general hobby 'law' that an error baseball card usually does not command any premium value," explains Bob Lemke, ed-itor and publisher of *Baseball Cards* and *Sports Collectors Digest* magazines.

"When the company that produced that card corrects the error and creates a card that varies from the first one, that can create some potentially higher dollar values. Many collectors will want both varieties of the cards, and it is likely that either the error card or the corrected version will have been printed in small quantities. That will make one of them more expensive.

"However, it usually is the corrected version that is scarcer. Again, error cards in and of themselves generally do not have a lot of value.

"Sometimes you'll find printing errors with wrong colors, or one side of the card is blank. I think those perhaps are a 'dark horse' area of investment [there's a slight chance they may become valuable].

"None of those kinds of cards have any real value except for ones with the major super stars on them. But I think that some day people are going to realize that, yes, these are very rare items. They just didn't get out [to the public] that often.

"Somewhere down the road errors could become a fairly popular area. It would be very challenging to collect, say, a 1986 Topps set of cards with blank backs. It could be done because there are enough blank back cards around, but just trying to accumulate those 792 cards would be a very challenging endeavor. Darn near impossible.

"But if error collecting ever catches on, the people who happen to have those things would be glad they held onto them," Lemke speculated.

Other baseball card experts are not so sure. Some advise collectors to completely ignore the error items.

"I don't like 'em," emphasizes Steve Goldberg of Dalton, Georgia. Goldberg is a dealer who buys and sells cards, stamps, and coins. He thinks that errors usually become a fad when they first come out. When a mistake is discovered the items are quickly bought up, but then a year later "you can't give 'em away," he says.

Dealer Kit Young of Vancouver, Washington, doesn't think much of errors, either. "They're all in the eyes of the beholder," he states.

"I would discourage kids from getting involved in errors. I think they should look at the error cards from the 1950s, such as the 1955 Bowmans. There is very little collector interest in them, very little value attached to them. Today's 'error' cards are much more plentiful and figure to have equally little value in future years. I think they're going to be really disappointed if they hope to resell them at a profit.

"A 1981 set of Donruss or Fleer errors doesn't mean a thing to the average dealer. It is not a good seller. It is not something I seek out to buy because I don't have buyers for it. So I really suggest that kids go for things they really enjoy—blue chip players, Hall of Famers, or rookies they enjoy," advises Young.

"But some of the errors have really been hyped up by some dealers who are trying to suggest the items are very scarce and therefore will be worth plenty of money some day in the future. Kids have to keep in mind that an item is only as valuable as the amount someone will pay you for it. There is a very limited market on most errors."

Bryan Durta, a dealer from Munster, Indiana, agrees. "The value doesn't seem to hold up on that stuff at all. It seems no one could care less about all the 1980s errors."

(An expression in stamp and coin collecting seems appropriate for baseball card errors: The only thing rarer than the item for sale is someone who wants to buy it!)

Jeff Fritsch of Stevens Point, Wisconsin still has some fondness for errors, but admits: "I used to think a lot more of them than I do today."

Fritsch believes that prior to 1981 error cards were more respected in the hobby. They were "something special" he explains, pointing to the 1979 Topps mistake with Bump Wills (#369-A and #369-B). Wills was erroneously identified as a member of the Toronto Blue Jays. The mistake was later corrected to match him with his fellow teammates on the Texas Rangers.

"It was a distinct error. You could put the cards next to each other and the mistake would pop right out at you. It was kind of neat to compare the two.

"But then starting in 1981 the card companies started correcting things, because they missed periods in punctuation or they listed 31 home runs instead of 32, and so then they issued another card to correct that on the back. Ever since then I don't think error cards are worth the paper they're printed on.

"The sad part is that young collectors are picking up on such things as minor mistakes in punctuation or statistics. I bet we get

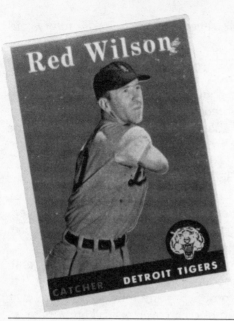

An intentional error: The background design of this 1958 Topps (#213) makes it appear that Detroit catcher Red Wilson has no arms!

(James A. Simek Photo. Copyright Topps Chewing Gum, Inc.)

five phone calls a week from kids who ask about some particular card and want to know if a typographical error is being corrected. They want to know if the cards will be worth anything.

"I can't blame people for wanting to make a buck, but I think they're losing the enjoyment of collecting by worrying about too many other things," Fritsch concludes.

Though many young collectors believe that the insignificant errors on their baseball cards will bring them instant fame and fortune, the reality is that most errors are not highly valued. Remember, if the error of fact has not been corrected by the cardmaker no additional value is usually attached to the card. Even if it has been corrected, sometimes the correct card is worth more than the error version.

Yet here's something to think about.

For hundreds of years generation after generation of sophisticated rare coin collectors shunned any error coins. They wanted only the finest available specimens of the mint master's art for their collections. So, mis-struck coins were tossed into circulation for spending money, not carefully saved and preserved for future generations.

Starting in the 1950s some collectors realized that error coins were useful for research. Knowing just how the error was made helped collectors learn more about the interesting process of minting coins. Suddenly, the ignored mistakes frequently described by prominent collectors as "freaks and oddities" found welcome homes in the collections of a small group of dedicated people who appreciated these previously rejected items.

Know what happened then? The values of many error coins zoomed up. In a few years, during the early 1960s, errors of all kinds became popular—so popular that a few unethical employees of the United States Mint began to "custom-make" some coins with dramatic mistakes. Those abuses were quickly eliminated.

(Some baseball card experts quietly believe that a few manufacturers actually may be producing errors cards on purpose to spark more interest in their products—and thus sell more cards.)

A small influential group of coin collectors still appreciate errors and are willing to pay substantial money to acquire off-center, multiple-strike and wrong planchet errors (for example, a one-cent piece accidently struck on a blank intended for the striking of a dime).

Billions and billions of coins are struck by the U.S. Mint every year so there will always be some mistakes, such as pennies that are 10 or 20 percent off-center. These are rather common and usually sell for a dollar or so each. But the earlier error coins that were not saved by discriminating collectors, such as Indian Head cents from the late 1800s and early 1900s that are mis-struck and still in gem brilliant red uncirculated condition, are worth hundreds of dollars each. If you can find them.

The larger the error and the earlier the date on the coin, the more valuable it probably will be.

What does this mean for baseball card collectors?

Perhaps, just perhaps, a few years down the road some collectors may begin to appreciate error cards. The wrong player's photo, the wrong stats, the wrong ink color or the wrong spelling of a player's name could become highly sought after by collectors looking for something different.

It's something to think about.

Sign of the Times

Autograph

collecting

It is not just the first and third base coaches and the catcher who are flashing signs at the ballpark. Virtually every player, coach and manager at one time or another is asked "to sign." Sign a game program, sign a baseball, sign a baseball card, even sign the wrapper in which a ballpark hot dog was contained. Fans love to get autographs!

During the warmup session before the game eager spectators hang over the dugout railing begging players to sign their names on anything handy. After the game fans wait outside the gate pleading for an autograph. At a national sports convention some autograph collectors began lining up before sunrise to get Mickey Mantle's signature.

American sports fans have a love affair not only with the athletes' feats, but with their hands when they are holding pens or pencils.

Autographed baseballs are a tradition. How many newspaper photographs have you seen of a popular player of yesterday or today taking time out to oblige the polite demands of children and adults in the stands by signing a ball?

This autographed photo of Babe Ruth was made into a collectors' postcard. It is just one of many items available with either an original autograph or a reproduction of the Babe's signature.
(Krause Publications Photo)

Now some fans are demanding even more. Collectors have been buying anything related to sports, with or without an autograph on it. Souvenir programs, cracked baseball bats, broken hockey sticks, smashed helmets, and even sweat-stained, used jerseys!

Babe Ruth was well-known for patiently honoring almost all requests for autographs, especially when youngsters were begging for a signature. (That's why so many items with the Babe's autograph are available.) Even today many baseball players are happy and honored to be asked for an autograph. Some players see the handwriting on the wall and are concerned their autographs have become a financially profitable industry for some dealers.

A few players are "charging" for autographs at the ballparks. If an adult asks for an autograph, the player may request that the fan immediately write a check for $5 or $10 made out to the player's favorite, non-profit charity. Other players are cashing in on the autograph demand by charging directly for their signatures when they attend "autograph sessions" at baseball card and sports collectibles shows and conventions.

When you glance through the hobby publication advertisements for upcoming shows you often find notices that certain current or former players will be available for autographs. Usually there is a charge for their signatures and that can range from $5 on up. It appears some former players are making a living off their handwriting these days.

Some collectors will pay a premium to obtain baseball cards autographed by the players depicted on the cards. Other collectors consider an autograph to be only defacing the card. Some buyers do not want "grafitti" covering an otherwise pristine card. You may find a buyer who will pay more for a card with an autograph, but it should be obvious that getting a card signed will limit the potential market for that card. Hobby experts advise: Don't have valuable cards autographed.

For the fans who do want autographs on cards or any other writing surface, there are plenty of opportunities to obtain them. You can purchase them outright from any of the numerous dealers who now handle autographed items, or you can obtain your own autographs either in person or through the mail.

One of the companies specializing in autograph sales is American Sports Collectibles (P.O. Box 475, Horsham, Pennsylvania 19044). Rather than "defacing" an otherwise valuable baseball card, the company produces "authentic autographs," framed signatures surrounded by a color photograph of the player and information about his lifetime statistics and major achievements. Prices for these items start at $29 each. Some critics claim it is only a promotional gimmick, but other hobby leaders praise the idea as a nice way to collect autographs without causing "damage" to otherwise collectible baseball cards.

If you want to obtain the signatures in person then you must go where the ballplayers go, either the ballparks or at other personal appearances. Spring training camps often are excellent places to chat with players and have them sign something for you. The atmosphere at the camp may be more relaxed than during the regular season. You may be able to talk with players before or after the games and even have an opportunity for some picture-taking as well as autographs.

Many Major League teams schedule autograph or photo days during the regular season. Take advantage of the "open house."

Major sports and card shows have been attracting may current and former super stars who will happily sign autographs for free or for a fee. Here is just a sample of some of the famous players who have attended recent major shows or the annual Hall of Fame weekend at Cooperstown, New York:

Eddie Stanky, Willie Mays, Bob Feller, Warren Spahn, Eddie Mathews, Ernie Banks, Johnny Mize, Hank Aaron, Stan Musial, Willy McCovey, Ralph Kiner, Bobby Doerr, Happy Chandler, Lefty Gomez, Ted Williams and Whitey Ford.

Until his death on October 3, 1986, former Boston Braves player Vince DiMaggio frequently held "reunions" with his baseball brothers wearing their old uniforms, Dom DiMaggio formerly of the Red Sox and Joe DiMaggio, the famous Yankee slugger. They often posed for fans' photos and would sign autographs.

The U.S. Postal Service can help you obtain autographs of present and past players. A handy book called *The Sport Americana Baseball Address List* provides names and mailing addresses for nearly every Major League baseball player since the World War I era (see the chapter on hobby publications). Many current players will sign autographs free if you mail them a baseball card or other item to sign. You can send it to the players in care of their teams. A list of Major League addresses is included below. Some fans have bragged of obtaining hundreds of autographs a year through the mail by writing directly to the players at the ballpark or team front office.

While many players are happy to sign and return the items as their time permits, a few players never acknowledge these requests. Some have other people (wives, girlfriends, secretaries, etc.) sign their names. One of the best ways to find out who is signing and who is not is to follow the comments of readers in hobby publications and also the feature articles about autographs in those newspapers and magazines. Authors Dave Miedema and Chris Burleson present a series of articles in *Baseball Cards* listing "who signs and who doesn't" and also giving warnings about apparently "ghost-signed" items.

If you mail something to a player to be autographed always remember to put the proper amount of postage on the envelope (you don't want the player to pay any postage due costs) and always include a stamped, self-addressed envelope. That way the player can sign your card and drop it into the envelope you've provided.

It usually is best to only send one or two items at a time to be autographed. How would you feel if you received a box filled with hundreds of cards to be autographed all at once? Also, some players seem to honor requests that obviously come from younger fans and tend to ignore autograph requests that are neatly typed on the letterhead stationery of a commercial enterprise.

Here is a list of mailing addresses for the American League and National League clubs. In some cases the address is the same as the club's stadium location. You can write to specific players at the address listed here for their team.

Remember to always include a stamped, self-addressed envelope (SASE) if you want a reply to your letter.

NATIONAL LEAGUE CLUBS

Atlanta Braves
Fulton County Stadium
521 Capitol Ave., S.W.
Atlanta, Georgia 30302

Chicago Cubs
Wrigley Field
1060 West Addison
Chicago, Illinois 60613

Cincinnati Reds
100 Riverfront Stadium
Cincinnati, Ohio 45202

Houston Astros
Astrodome
Post Office Box 288
Houston, Texas 77001

Los Angeles Dodgers
1000 Elysian Park Ave.
Los Angeles, California 90012

Montreal Expos
Post Office Box 500
Station "M"
Montreal, Quebec H1V 3P2
Canada

New York Mets
Shea Stadium
Flushing, New York 11368

Philadelphia Phillies
Post Office Box 7575
Philadelphia, Pennsylvania 19101

Pittsburgh Pirates
Post Office Box 7000
Three Rivers Stadium
Pittsburgh, Pennsylvania 15212

St. Louis Cardinals
Busch Memorial Stadium
250 Stadium Plaza
St. Louis, Missouri 63102

San Diego Padres
9449 Friars Road
San Diego, California 92108

San Francisco Giants
Candlestick Park
San Francisco, California 94124

AMERICAN LEAGUE CLUBS

Baltimore Orioles
Memorial Stadium
Baltimore, Maryland 21218

Boston Red Sox
24 Yawkey Way
Fenway Park
Boston, Massachusetts 02215

California Angels
2000 State College Blvd.
Anaheim, California 92806

Chicago White Sox
Comiskey Park
324 West 35th Street
Chicago, Illinois 60616

Cleveland Indians
Cleveland Stadium
Cleveland, Ohio 44114

Detroit Tigers
Tiger Stadium
Detroit, Michigan 48216

Kansas City Royals
One Royal Way
Kansas City, Missouri 64129

Milwaukee Brewers
Milwaukee County Stadium
Milwaukee, Wisconsin 53214

Minnesota Twins
501 Chicago Ave., South
Minneapolis, Minnesota 55415

New York Yankees
Yankee Stadium
Bronx, New York 10451

Oakland Athletics
Oakland-Alameda County Coliseum
Oakland, California 94621

Seattle Mariners
Post Office Box 4100
Seattle, Washington 98104

Texas Rangers
Post Office Box 1111
Arlington, Texas 76010

Toronto Blue Jays
Box 7777
Adelaide Street Post Office
Toronto, Ontario M5C 2K7
Canada

Preserving the Past

B aseball cards help us preserve the past. The thrills of our favorite players and teams, the highlights and the lowlights of actions both on and off the field, are easily remembered merely by glancing at a card. Holding a Roger Clemens card may evoke personal recollections of watching his Most Valuable Player performances during Boston's pennant-winning 1986 season. Seeing a slightly-faded card of "Shoeless" Joe Jackson provides a history lesson on the Chicago "Black Sox" World Series scandal of 1919, and, perhaps, thoughts of what might have been if the South Carolina slugger (.356 lifetime average) had not been permanently barred from baseball in 1920 by the game's first Commissioner, Kenesaw Mountain Landis.

Baseball cards are sports history you can hold in your hands.

History must be carefully preserved. That means your baseball cards, particularly those with even the slightest potential for increase in value, should be protected from potential damage. Those cards already with significant values must be placed in protective holders and treated with the same love and care collectors and investors provide for rare coins and postage stamps.

Standing in the aisle at a local weekend card show or at the neighborhood card shop you'll see youngsters and adults thumbing through boxes of loose cards or stashing just-purchased cards in a back pocket. Each small fingerprint, each minor crease or slight "dog-ear" wear on the cardboard layers, may eventually bring down the value of that card.

You don't need surgical gloves to handle baseball cards; just use common sense and care. Handle them with clean hands, don't cough or sneeze on them, and house them in a protective holder.

If you purchase entire sets at a time, the cards will come in a box. This makes a nice home for them as long as they are not exposed for years to excessively high humidity or put in a place where the cards could be crushed by a heavy object or submerged in a basement flood.

(Frequently, when you see baseball cards produced for Venezuela during the late 1950s and 1960s the cards are only in fair to very good condition. The climate of the country, and the common method of housing the cards by many of the collectors, resulted in the deterioration of the cards. Many of the collectors simply pasted or taped them into scrapbooks.)

Cards purchased just for the fun of it should be used just for the fun of it. How many childhood hours were spent lashing small stacks of cards together with rubber bands and competitively tossing the decks onto sidewalk cracks, or swapping cards back and forth with friends? Current cards usually are good casual enjoyment.

Serious collecting demands serious attention to making sure the cherished cards are carefully preserved for your enjoyment—and importantly—the enjoyment of future generations of baseball card collectors.

Fortunately, many kinds of protective holders are available, permitting collectors and investors to see and enjoy their cards and preserve them at the same time.

There are "sleeves" into which individual cards can be placed. The card can be easily held, seen on both sides, and placed in another sturdy container for storage while still in the transparent holder. Manufacturers of these individual-card holders produce containers to accommodate baseball cards of various sizes. One of the best brands is Protecto's "Card-Gards," polyethylene holders that usually are sold in lots of 100 or more and cost about a penny or less each.

Polyethelene, polypropylene and vinyl sheets are available at about 10 to 15 cents each that usually accommodate nine cards per page. The pages can be placed in three-ring binders for easy viewing and storage of the cards. Some binder albums will hold 100 or more of these pages.

Extremely valuable cards might merit thick plexiglass holders that screw tightly together with an individual card safely sandwiched in the middle. These fancy holders sell for about $5 and up. It doesn't make sense to house a $2 card in a $5 holder, but any collector fortunate enough to have a mint condition 1949 Bowman Satchell Paige (#224) card might consider special protection for their treasure.

For storing a team-at-a-time, you can purchase hard plastic card cases that flip open just like an audio cassette tape box. These card cases are available in sizes that will hold anywhere from 15 to 100 cards. Full-year sets can be housed in heavy duty construction, 200 pound test strength cardboard boxes that will hold between 100 cards and 3,200. Collectors who frequently like to examine their cards stored in a cardboard box would be smart to place the cards in individual sleeves for greater protection.

Some coin, stamp, and paper money collectors learned a devastating lesson in the 1970s. Polyvinyl chloride (PVC) holders frequently were used to store their collections. Unfortunately, PVC can chemically break down, releasing small amounts of gas that can leave a greenish residue on items stored in the holders. The damage can be financially fatal.

Avoid PVC holders even for short-term storage of baseball cards. Holders made of polyethelene, polypropylene, or Mylar are much safer.

The small price to pay for the proper protection of your cards could be the smartest long-term investment you'll make in the hobby.

The Sports Pages

There are no nationwide baseball card clubs, no organization that you can join for weekly, monthly or yearly conventions similar to those conducted by the American Philatelic Society and the American Numismatic Association. Without an organization like the APS or the ANA no nationwide society holds seminars on baseball cards. In fact, virtually no local card clubs are around.

Yet, numerous opportunities exist to meet other collectors and dealers face-to-face. A major card show is produced every year under the banner of the "National Sports Collector's Convention," and virtually every weekend local card shows are being held in the major cities.

The way to learn about these shows, these opportunities to buy, sell, swap and educate yourself about cards, is to read the hobby publications. Just as astute baseball followers will pore over page after page of *Inside Sports, Sports Illustrated, The Sporting News* and *Baseball Digest*, astute collectors follow their favorite hobby in the pages of publications such as *Beckett Baseball Card Monthly* and *Baseball Cards*.

In addition to interesting articles about cards for both beginners and advanced collectors, these publications list upcoming card shows and conventions, providing important information about the dates, hours and locations of the events, how many dealers will have tables set up for business, and if an admission fee is charged.

The "Show Schedule" sections usually are arranged chronologically, making it easy to quickly find the next upcoming event closest to your hometown.

The following is a list of veteran and rookie hobby publications and a few important books for the serious collector or investor of baseball cards. Remember the words of the German writer Goethe: "Knowledge is power."

Baseball Card Digest
22203 John R Road
Hazel Park, Michigan 48030

A relative newcomer to the hobby publications field that is aiming to provide readers with information about new card issues as well as the classics. Published six times a year. Single copy price is $1.25. One year subscription $5.75; two years $10.50.

Baseball Card Investment Report
American Card Exchange
3822 Campus Drive, Suite 134
Newport Beach, California 92660

A monthly newsletter with baseball card market analysis, buying and selling strategies, and "bid" and "ask" prices for more than 300 of the most popular investor-quality cards in the marketplace. *Baseball Card Investment Report* is the product of card dealer Tony Galovich and rare coin dealers David Hall and Van Simmons. A complimentary copy is available for the asking. Write to the above address for additional information about subscriptions.

Baseball Card News
700 East State Street
Iola, Wisconsin 54990

A monthly newspaper covering all types of sports collectibles with emphasis on baseball cards, autographs, photos, yearbooks, ticket stubs, and other sports souvenirs of baseball, football, basketball, hockey, boxing, basketball and some non-sports areas, too. Subscriptions: One year $15; two years $27; three years $38.

Baseball Cards
700 East State Street
Iola, Wisconsin 54990

Underscoring the tremendous increase in card collecting, this publication switched in 1987 from producing four issues a year to becoming a monthly magazine. Each issue has a lengthy baseball card price guide and in addition to about a half dozen special articles about cards and players there are interesting regular features such as the "Collector Question & Answer" department. Frequent use of full-color photographs of various cards and players make the magazine even more lively. Single issue newsstand cover price is $2.50 per copy. Subscriptions for 12 issues (one year) are $11.95.

Beckett Baseball Card Monthly
3410 MidCourt, Suite 110
Carrollton, Texas 75006

This is a publication produced with great love by the prominent collector and baseball card researcher, Dr. James Beckett. The magazine is issued every month except for combined November-December and January-February issues. Its articles give a sense of historical perspective to the game of baseball and the cards that reflect that history. A regular feature is the "Weather Report," a "temperature" ranking of which players are hot and which are not, according to readers. (Sometimes a player, such as Pete Rose, gets ranked on both lists because some readers think he's hot, others claim he's cold.) Naturally, the centerpiece of the magazine is an updated card price guide compiled by the very respected Dr. Beckett and his staff. Cover price is $2.50. Subscriptions are one year (10 issues) $17.95; two years (20 issues) $31.95; three years (30 issues) $41.95; and four years (40 issues) $49.95.

Current Card Prices
433 North Windsor Ave.
Brightwaters, New York 11718

Editor Richard Schawaroch tracks average prices of baseball cards by surveying over 300 dealers across the country. Nothing fancy in C.C.P., but a quick guide to Bowman, Topps and other post-World War II card issues. (There also is a similar C.C.P. publication that tracks football and hockey cards.) Sample copy is $2.50. Subscriptions for baseball issues are one year (12 issues) $19.95; two years (24 issues) $37.95. (The football/hockey publication is also $2.50 for a sample copy; one year with four issues is $6.95; two years with eight issues is $12.95.)

Guide to Pre Rookie Prices
Cornelius Collectibles
102 2nd Avenue
Bagley, Iowa 50026

A new, quarterly publication that tracks prices of about 400 Minor League card sets and provides news about the best current young prospects in the minors who could become the next super star rookies in the majors. Sample copy $2.50. One year subscription (4 issues) $8.50.

Sports Collectors Digest
700 East State Street
Iola, Wisconsin 54990

Another outstanding publication from the dedicated hobby writers and editors at Krause Publications in the small northern Wisconsin community of Iola. With an updated price guide in each issue every two weeks, those writers and publisher Bob Lemke keep the keyboards and calculators busy. Each thick issue runs about 250 pages and is filled with advertisements and late-breaking news about new card issues, readers' questions (and the editor's answers), feature articles and usually lots of black and white photos of cards and ballplayers. S.C.D. is the hobby's largest and oldest publication. Single copy price is $2.50. Subscriptions are six months (13 issues) $12.95; one year (26 issues) $24.95; two years (52 issues) $46.50; and three years (78 issues) $67.00.

The Old Judge
c/o Lew Lipset
P.O. Box 137
Centereach, New York 11720

An informative newsletter that provides an update for the very important *Encyclopedia of Baseball Cards* and provides comments on hobby trends, as well as supplying price guide information on pre-World War II baseball cards. The publication's name, of course, refers to the Old Judge cigarettes that launched the baseball card craze a century ago. One year subscription (four issues plus two price updates) $7.00.

Tuff-Stuff
Box 1637
Glen Allen, Virginia 23060

Another relative newcomer to the hobby field. One year subscription (12 issues) $6.99; two years (24 issues) $10.99.

Casual and serious collectors should add a few important research books to their home libraries.

The Official Price Guide to Baseball Cards is the number one annual guide to the collecting, buying, selling and swapping of baseball cards. A paperback book with more than 400 pages containing over 100,000 price listings for baseball cards produced by major manufacturers since 1948. The author of this important annual reference work is Dr. James Beckett. While the prices of many cards may be outdated not long after the book is published each year (the monthly and twice-monthly magazines and newsletters can provide more current price information), this particular book is a vital source of data on card issues, card numbers, card varieties and solid, basic information on baseball cards in general. No serious collector can afford to not own a copy at only $4.95 each at book stores and baseball card shops.

The American Card Catalog, published in 1960, established the guidelines for putting cards into specific categories, such as "tobacco" cards issued with cigarette products, etc. Virtually all collectors and dealers now follow the ACC numbering system for cards.

A fabulous "coffee table" book, *Topps Baseball Cards: A 35*

Year History 1951-1985, puts full-color illustrations of all 22,000 Topps cards from that time period at your fingertips in 1,300 pages. The book usually sells for about $75, but some bookstores and card dealers have offered copies for as little as $59 each. It is a delightful way to finally own an entire Topps 1952 set of cards!

A three-volume set of the *Encyclopedia of Baseball Cards* has been produced tracing the history of cards from the 19th century (volume one $9.95) to the early gum and candy cards (volume two $10.95) and through the 20th century tobacco cards (volume three $12.95). They are sold through Lew Lipset (see above *The Old Judge* address and add $1.50 per order for postage charges) and other dealers, such as Beckett Publications.

Beckett also offers collectors many other very useful books that are featured in ads in each issue of *Beckett Baseball Card Monthly.* Among the handiest are *The Sport Americana Baseball Card Team Checklist* ($8.95), *The Sport Americana Alphabetical Baseball Card Checklist* ($8.95) and *The Sport Americana Baseball Address List* with mailing addresses for virtually all active and retired Major League players (fourth edition $9.95). These books and other price guides are available from Beckett Publications, 3410 MidCourt, Suite 110, Carrollton, Texas 75006. Add $1 per book for postage.

THE TENTH INNING. What is the future of baseball cards as their second century of nationwide enjoyment gets underway?

"I think the growth will continue because innovation will continue," states Donald Peck, president of Fleer Corp.

I agree, Mr. Peck. And I add one more thing: the fun of baseball cards will continue, too.

Play ball!

OTHER BOOKS BY AUTHOR:

Breaking Into Broadcasting,
Bonus Books, Chicago, Illinois